Literacy

Anthology

Compiled by Margaret Stillie

This selection copyright © Margaret Stillie 1999

Illustrations copyright © STP 1999

The acknowledgements on p254
constitute an extension of this copyright page.

All rights reserved. No part of this publication may
be reproduced or transmitted in any form or by
any means, electronic or mechanical, including
photocopy, recording or any information storage
and retrieval system, without permission in
writing from the publisher or under licence from
the Copyright Licensing Agency Limited. Further
details of such licences (for reprographic
reproduction) may be obtained from the Copyright
Licensing Agency Limited of 90 Tottenham Court
Road, London W1P OLP.

First published by
Stanley Thornes Publishers Ltd
Ellenborough House
Wellington Street
Cheltenham
GL50 1YW

00 01 02 03 04 \ 10 9 8 7 6 5 4 3 2

A catalogue record for this book is available from
the British Library

ISBN 0-7487-4822-9

Designed by Oxford Designers and Illustrators/STP.
Page make-up by StoreyBooks, Honiton, Devon.
Printed and bound in Italy
by G. Canale & C.S.p.A., Borgaro T.se, Turin.

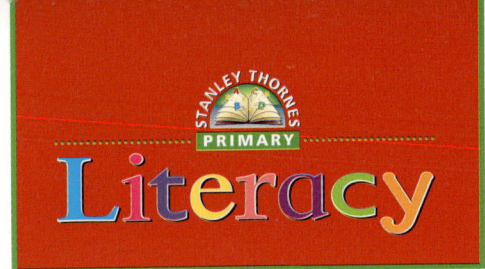

Contents

Term 1
Unit 1	"Autumn Song" *by Ted Hughes*	**6**
	"River Winding" *by Charlotte Zolotow*	**7**
Unit 2	Mog and Bumble *by Catherine Robinson*	**8**
Unit 3	"Orders of the Day" *by John Cunliffe*	**12**
	"Juster and Waiter" *by Michael Rosen*	**13**
	"If you don't put your Shoes On" *by Michael Rosen*	**14**
Unit 4	William's Problems *by Shirley Isherwood*	**16**
Unit 5	Tudors and Stuarts *by Katerini Siliprandi and Sheila Watson*	**22**
Unit 7	Leave me Alone *by David Williams*	**38**
Unit 8	A Green Harvest *by Wes Magee*	**46**
Unit 9	Anne Frank *by Wayne Jackson*	**52**
Unit 10	When Hitler Stole Pink Rabbit *by Judith Kerr*	**58**
Unit 11	Let's Celebrate Winter *by Rhoda Nottridge*	**72**
	"Light the Festive Candles" *by Aileen Fisher*	**76**
	"Crown of Light Festival" *by David Bateson*	**77**

Term 2
Unit 1	Seymour Finds a Home *by Dyan Sheldon*	**78**
Unit 2	"Eskimo Lullaby" *Anon*	**82**
	"The Good Little Girl" *by A.A.Milne*	**82**
	"Quartermasters Stores" *Anon*	**84**
	"Allie" *by Robert Graves*	**86**
	"My Bonnie" *Anon*	**87**
	"Praise Song of the Wind" *Anon (Teleut People of Siberia)*	**88**
	"The Panther Roars" *Anon (Gond, India)*	**89**
Unit 3	Spook Spotting *by Mary Hooper*	**90**
Unit 4	The Conker as Hard as a Diamond *by Chris Powling*	**96**

Unit 5	Fishing Boats	**106**
	Fish	**108**
	Whales *by Norman Barrett*	**110**
Unit 6	A Fish of the World *by Terry Jones*	**112**
Unit 7	"Colin" *by Allan Ahlberg*	**116**
	"Please Mrs Butler" *by Allan Ahlberg*	**118**
	"A Schoolmaster's Admonition" *Anon (1625)*	**119**
	"Demeanour" *Anon (c. 1525)*	**120**
	"The Dunce" *by Walter de la Mare*	**121**
	"The Outing" *by Michael Rosen*	**121**
Unit 8	The Knowhow Book of Print and Paint *by Heather Avery and Anne Cwardi*	**128**
Unit 9	The Not-Very-Nice-Prince *by Pamela Oldfield*	**132**
Unit 10	Savitri and Satyavan *by Madhur Jaffrey*	**138**
Unit 11	Once there were no Pandas *by Margaret Greaves*	**152**
Unit 12	"Brazilian Footballer" *by Faustin Charles*	**158**
	"Hurricane" *by Dionne Brand*	**159**
	"Isn't My Name Magical" *by James Berry*	**159**
	"Chicken Dinner" *by Valerie Bloom*	**161**

Term 3

Unit 1	Cheating *by Susan Shreve*	**162**
Unit 2	"Riddles in Rhyme" *Anon*	**168**
	"Jelly on the Plate" *Anon*	**169**
	"BED!" *by Joni Akinrele*	**171**
	"Haiku" *by Margaret Stillie*	**172**
	"Centipede's Song" *by Roald Dahl*	**172**
	"WHY?" *by Marcus Lewis*	**175**
Unit 3	Hey, Danny! *by Robin Klein*	**176**
Unit 5	"I Did a Bad Thing Once" *by Allan Ahlberg*	**184**
	"In the Playground" *by Stanley Cook*	**184**
	"The Gang" *by Allan Ahlberg*	**185**
	"Sometimes God" *by Allan Ahlberg*	**186**
	"My Gerbil" *by Beatrice Higgins*	**187**
	"Limericks" *by Gelett Burgess and Michael Palin*	**189**
	"Eddie and the Gerbils" *by Michael Rosen*	**190**
Unit 6	Lost – One Pair of Legs *by Joan Aiken*	**194**
Unit 8	A Necklace of Raindrops *by Joan Aiken*	**204**
Unit 9	The Slave who became Chief *by Charles Mungoshi*	**216**
Unit 10	A Chinese Fairy Tale *retold by Laurence Houseman*	**228**
Unit 11	The Girl Who Stayed for Half a Week *by Gene Kemp*	**242**

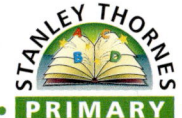

Literacy

Anthology extracts

Autumn Song

There came a day that caught the summer
Wrung its neck
Plucked it
And ate it.

Now what shall I do with the trees?
The day said, the day said.
Strip them bare, strip them bare.
Let's see what is really there.

And what shall I do with the sun?
The day said, the day said.
Roll him away till he's cold and small.
He'll come back rested if he comes back at all.

And what shall I do with the birds?
The day said, the day said.
The birds I've frightened, let them flit,
I'll hang out pork for the brave tomtit.

And what shall I do with the seed?
The day said, the day said.
Bury it deep, see what it's worth.
See if it can stand the earth.

What shall I do with the people?
The day said, the day said.

Stuff them with apple and blackberry pie –
They'll love me then till the day they die.

There came this day and he was autumn.
His mouth was wide
And red as a sunset.
His tail was an icicle.

Ted Hughes

River Winding

Rain falling, what things do you grow?
Snow melting, where do you go?
Wind blowing, what trees do you know?
River winding, where do you flow?

Charlotte Zolotow

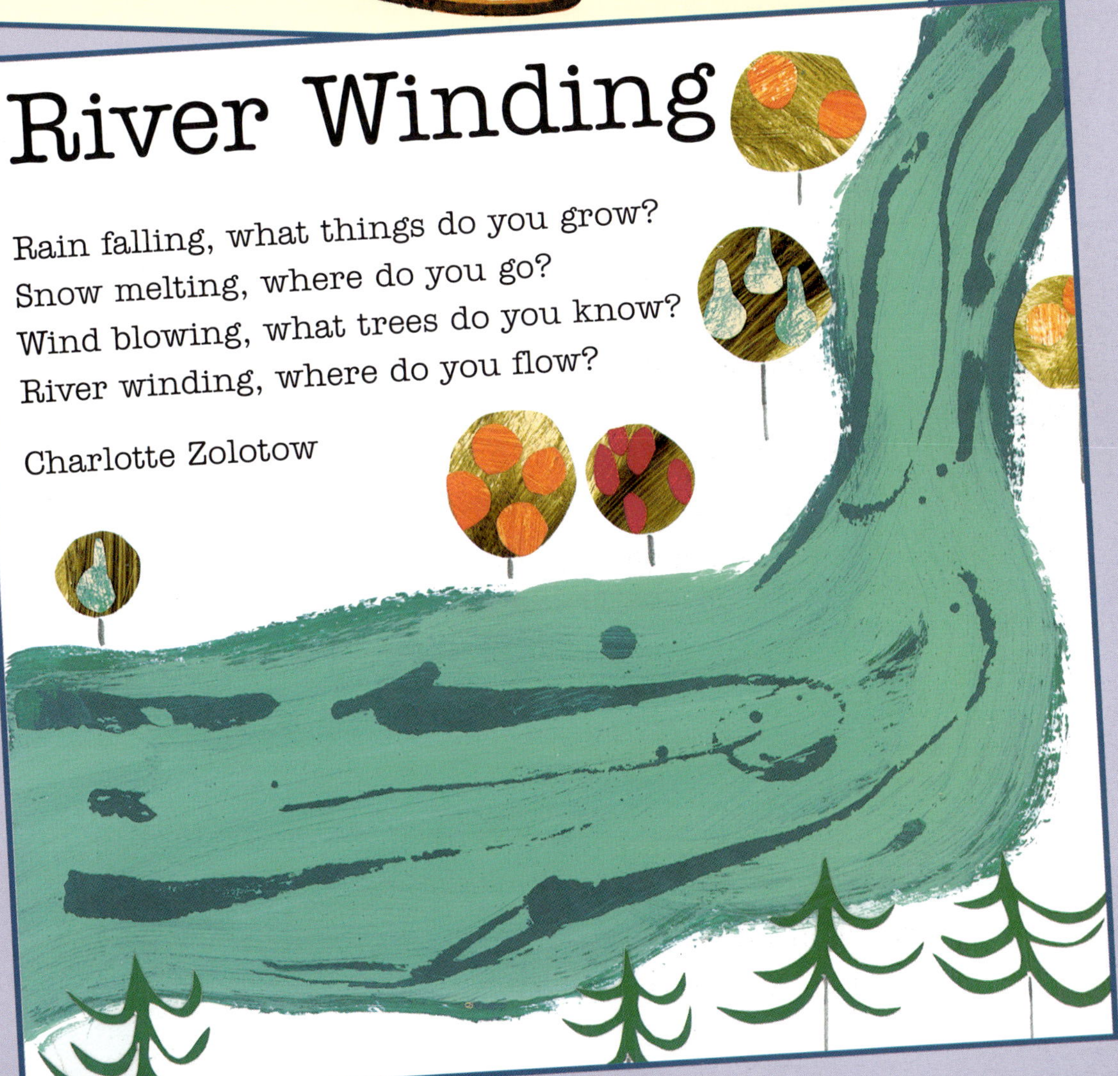

Term 1 | Unit 2

Mog and Bumble

by Catherine Robinson

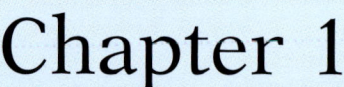

Chapter 1

Mog came to live with the Smiths a long time ago. They found him fast asleep among the packing cases and boxes when they first moved in to their house. It was snowing, and they hadn't the heart to put him out again. Then Mum gave him a saucer of milk, and that was that; he was there for good. If he'd once had another home, he never went back to it, and nobody ever came looking for him.

All this had happened such a long time ago that Sarah couldn't remember a time when Mog wasn't living with them.

"I can," said William. "I remember before he came."

Sarah scoffed. "You can't! You weren't even born then."

Sarah was Mog's little girl. They were special friends. Mog would even let Sarah tickle his tummy, which Mum said a lot of cats wouldn't put up with. And in return, Sarah would tell him what a wonderful, beautiful, extra-special cat he was.

He wasn't really. He was just an ordinary tabby cat with a white bib and paws. He was a bit battered about the

ears, because he didn't like other cats very much and was always getting into fights. And over the last winter or two the Smiths had noticed him limping.

"He's got rheumatism," Dad told them. "He's getting old." But he was still beautiful to Sarah.

Chapter 2

One day, Mum and Dad and Sarah and William all went for a ride in the car. Mum and Dad wouldn't tell Sarah and William where they were going. They just smiled at each other from time to time.

At last, the car drew up outside a big house. Sarah could hear masses and masses of dogs, all barking at once.

"Why have we come here?" she asked Mum. "What is this place, anyway?"

"It's the RSPCA," Mum told her, still smiling. "They look after lost dogs and cats, and find homes for them."

William started to jump around with excitement. "Yah-hoo!" he shouted. He knew why they'd come. "We're getting a dog! We're getting a dog!" And Sarah could see from Mum and Dad's faces that it was true.

William had been asking for a dog for ages, but Mum and Dad had never said anything except "We'll see." Sarah hated it when they said that. She knew it usually meant "No." But this time, it must have meant "Yes."

Term 1 | Unit 2

At first, Sarah didn't like the idea very much. She wasn't sure how Mog would feel about having a dog around the place. But when she saw the dogs, she changed her mind.

As the Smiths walked up and down the concrete paths, trying to choose one, all the dogs came right up to the wire netting. They wagged their tails and pressed their wet noses through the holes in the fence. Some of them even jumped up and down, eager to be chosen as William's dog. Sarah would have liked to have taken them all home, but she knew they couldn't. She didn't like to think about what might happen to the dogs they didn't choose.

William finally picked one. It was a puppy, with soft-looking fluffy brown fur. One ear stood up straight while

10

the other sort of flopped over one eye. The other eye had a white patch around it.

"Isn't he cute?" William yelled with pleasure.

Dad agreed he was. "Look at him bumbling along; he knows he's going home with you!"

Mum and Dad sorted things out with the RSPCA man. Then they drove home, with the new puppy on William's lap in the back of the car.

"You'll have to think of a name for him," Mum told William. "How about Patch? That's a good name."

William shook his head. "No. His name's Bumble."

Orders of the Day

Get up!
Get washed!
Eat your breakfast!
That's my mum,
Going on and on and on and on and on . . .

Sit down!
Shut up!
Get on with your work!
That's my teacher,
Going on and on and on and on and on . . .

Come here!
Give me that!
Go away!
That's my big sister,
Going on and on and on and on and on . . .

Get off!
Stop it!
Carry me!
That's my little sister,
Going on and on and on and on and on . . .

Boss
Boss
Boss

They do it all day.
Sometimes I think I'll run away,
But I don't know
Where to go.

The only one who doesn't do it,
Is my old gran.
She says,
"Would you like to get washed?"
Or,
"Would you like to sit on
　　　　this chair?"
And she listens to what I say.

People say she spoils me,
And that she's old-fashioned.
I think it's the others that spoil;
Spoil every day.
And I wish more people were
　　　　old-fashioned,
. . . like my gran.

John Cunliffe

Juster and Waiter

My mum had nicknames for me
　and my brother.
One of us she called Waiter
　and the other she called Juster.
It started like this:
she'd say, "Lend me a hand with
　the washing up
will you, you two?"
and I'd say, "Just a minute,
　Mum."
and my brother'd say
"Wait a minute, Mum."
"There you go again" – she'd say,
"Juster and Waiter."

Michael Rosen

If you don't put your shoes on

If you don't put your shoes on before I count fifteen then we won't go to the woods to climb the chestnut tree one
    But I can't find them
Two
    I can't
They're under the sofa three
    No
    Oh yes
Four five six
    Stop – they've got knots they've got knots
You should untie the laces when you take your shoes off seven
    Will you do one shoe while I do the other then?
Eight but that would be cheating
    Please
All right
    It always . . .
Nine
    It always sticks – I'll use my teeth
Ten
    It won't it won't
    It has – look
Eleven
    I'm not wearing any socks
Twelve
    Stop counting stop counting. Mum where are my

socks mum?
They're in your shoes. Where you left them.
    I didn't

Thirteen
    Oh they're inside out and upside down and
    bundled up

Fourteen
    Have you done the knot on the shoe you were . .

Yes
 Put it on the right foot
    But socks don't have right and wrong foot

The shoes silly
Fourteen and a half
    I am I am – wait
    Don't go to the woods without me
    Look that's one shoe already

Fourteen and threequarters
    There
You haven't tied the bows yet
    We could do them on the way there
No we won't fourteen and seven eighths
    Help me then
    You know I'm not fast at bows

Fourteen and fifteen sixteeeenths
    A single bow is all right isn't it?

Fifteen we're off
    See I did it.
    Didn't I?

Michael Rosen

Term 1 | Unit 4

William's Problems

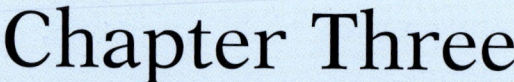

by Shirley Isherwood

Chapter Three

The next day was just as bad. At school, William got all his b's and d's the wrong way round.

His teacher tried to help him.

"Draw the stick and then the circle to make a b," he said. "And draw the circle and then the stick to make a d."

But still William couldn't remember which way was which when he came to write the letters down.

"William Barnes is *stupid*," said a boy in William's class.

"No, I'm *not*," said William, and he went home in a bad temper, feeling very unhappy.

At home he found that Matthew was in a bad temper too, because he was tired after being woken up in the night by Grandfather's tuba. He was crying, and William's mother was trying to soothe him.

She wasn't in a very good temper either, and she didn't seem to listen when William tried to tell her about the b's and d's going wrong, and about being called stupid. And it was all because of his grandfather, thought William.

William went out into the garden, and decided that everything was awful, and that he would run away from home. He ran off down the street, round the corner, and into the park.

But, once in the park, there didn't seem to be anywhere else to go. He went into the playground, but there was no one on the swings. Everyone was at home, having tea. William wandered round and round, feeling lonely, a bit frightened, and very hungry.

Then he began to run again – and as he went down the broad path, he saw his grandfather.

He was sitting on a bench, and when he saw William, he stuck out his walking stick, so suddenly that William almost fell over it.

"What are *you* doing here?" said William's grandfather.

"I'm running away!" said William.

"Why?" said his grandfather.

"I've got problems," said William.

"So have I," said his grandfather.

William was surprised. He had never thought of his grandfather having problems. He sat down on the bench and looked at him.

"What's your problem?" said William's grandfather.

William didn't like to say, "It's you!" So he said, "I can't get b's and d's the right way round."

"That's an easy problem to solve," said William's

Term 1 | Unit 4

grandfather, and he took a notebook and a pencil from his pocket. "All you have to do," he said, "is draw a little bed, like this."

He drew a bed, with the stick of the b making the head of the bed, and the stick of the d making the foot. The circles of the letters made the middle of the bed.

Then he drew a little stick-man on the bed, with his head on the b and his feet on the d.

William took the notebook and the pencil and turned to a clean page.

Then he thought of the little bed, and made the b and d. They were the right way round, said his grandfather.

So William thought of other words with the letters b and d, and thought of the little bed and got the letters right. It was wonderful. One of his problems was solved.

Grandfather put away the notebook and they both got up and began to walk down the path.

William turned to look at his grandfather. "What's your problem?" he said.

"Living in someone else's house," said his grandfather. "That's my problem."

Chapter Four

William was more surprised than ever. William's problem was that his grandfather was living with him. And now his grandfather said that *his* problem was living with William.

They both had the same problem really, thought William.

"Don't you *like* living with us?" he asked.

"It's fine!" said his grandfather. "It just takes a little getting used to."

They turned round, and began to make their way back home for tea.

"Were you seen and not heard when you were a little boy?" said William, as they went.

"No," said his grandfather, "and I don't suppose that you will be – will you?"

"No," said William.

"Then I'll stop asking you," said his grandfather.

They went a little further, and then his grandfather spoke again.

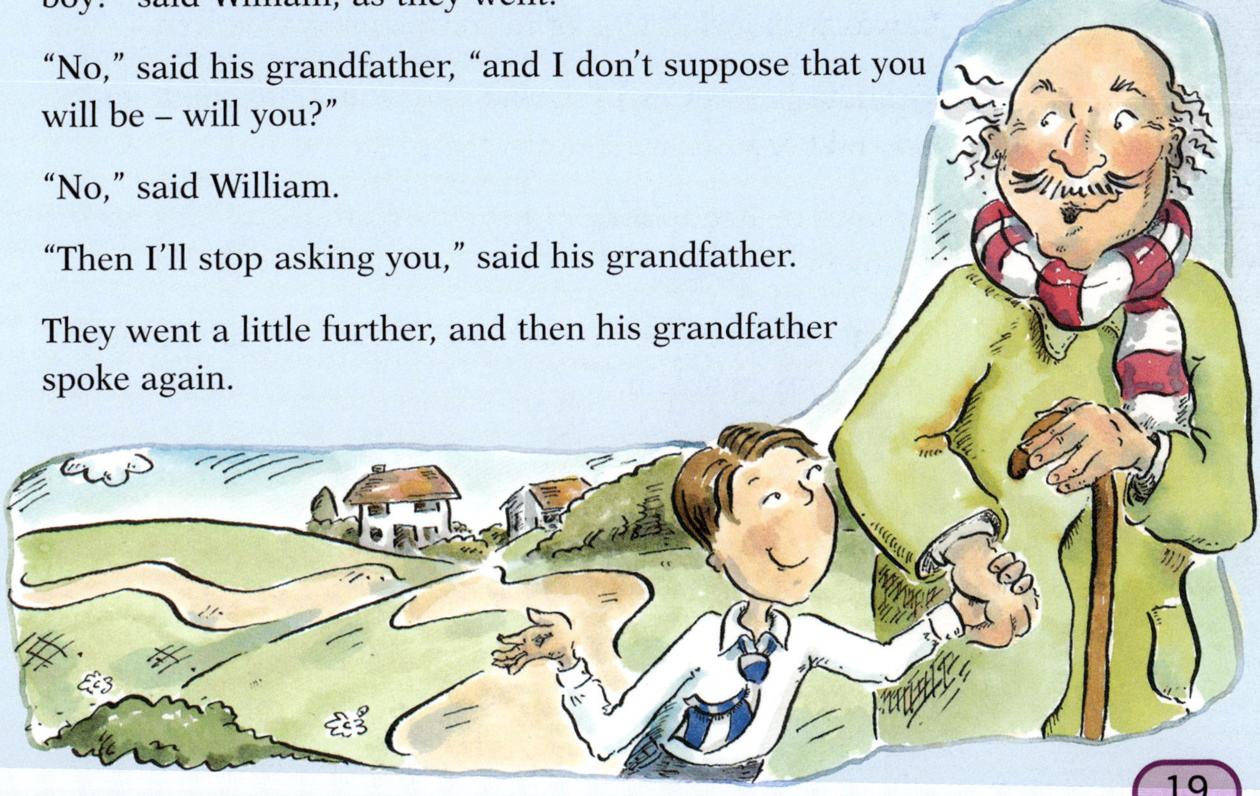

"Sorry you got booted out of your room, William," he said.

"That's all right," said William. "I'll get used to it."

But there was still the problem of the tuba-playing. Everyone had a talk about it after tea – and it was William who solved the problem.

"Why don't you play in the morning?" he said. "Everyone's awake then, so the noise wouldn't matter."

"What a good idea!" said William's grandfather.

So they asked Mrs Dart and Mr Humber if they would mind if Grandfather played his tuba in the morning, and they both said, "Not at all!"

The next morning, before he went to school, William heard his grandfather play the lion song, and the walloping seal waltz. He whistled the tunes all the way to school.

In the afternoon his teacher asked everyone to write about someone they knew. William decided he would write about his grandfather.

"My grandfather has come to live with us," he wrote. "I didn't think I liked him at first. It gives you a bad feeling when someone lives with you, and you don't like them. But now I like him a lot better. I think he likes me. He still shouts when he talks, but my mother says he's always done that, so he isn't going to stop. He stares at you a lot, but I think that's just because he likes to have a good look at things."

William's teacher liked what William had written. "It's very good, William," he said. "And you've got all your b's and d's the right way round. Well done!"

"No problem!" said William.

Term 1 | Unit 5

Tudors and Stuarts

by Katrini Siliprandi and Sheila Watson

Henry Becomes King

On 19 July, 1545, the *Mary Rose*, a warship, sank near Portsmouth on the south coast of England. Henry VIII, the King of England, watched with horror from the shore. The *Mary Rose* was one of about sixty ships, preparing to do battle with the French. It had holes in its sides for its giant guns, and was probably trying to sail with these uncovered. Water rushed through the holes into the lower deck, causing the *Mary Rose* to capsize. Almost all the crew of 500 men 'drowned like ratten' [rats].

A page from the 'Anthony Roll' of 1546, showing the *Mary Rose*. The roll was a list of all Henry VIII's ships and their equipment. The roll was published one year after the sinking of the *Mary Rose*.

By that date, 1545, Henry VIII had been king for thirty-six years. Many changes had taken place during this time. He had married six women. All the monasteries had been closed down. At the start of his reign Henry had been very rich, but now he was almost bankrupt. He had been handsome, but now he was enormously fat with painful legs.

Henry was born on 28 June, 1491, in the royal palace at Greenwich in Kent, 8 km south-east of London. His mother was Elizabeth of York, his father was the first Tudor king, Henry VII. He grew up with his mother, his older brother Arthur and his sisters, Margaret and Mary. Most of his childhood was spent at the royal palaces near London: Greenwich, Eltham and the palace of Sheen, later renamed Richmond.

An artist's impression of how Henry looked as a child.

Henry, aged about thirty-six. When he was young people said he was the most handsome prince in Europe.

IMPORTANT DATES

1491	Henry VIII born.
1501	Henry VIII's brother, Arthur, marries Catherine of Aragon.
1502	Arthur dies.
1509	Henry VII dies.
	Henry VIII marries Catherine of Aragon.
	Henry VIII crowned King of England.

Term 1 | Unit 5

The Early Years

Crowds cheered as Elizabeth I went in procession through the city of London on the day before her **coronation** in January 1559. Seated on a **litter**, wearing a long cloak of gold tissue, the young Queen was showered with **nosegays** and bunches of herbs. After her coronation, a great banquet was held in Westminster Hall.

The Queen's champion, Sir Edward Dymoke, offered to fight anyone who challenged Elizabeth's right to the throne. No one did, but many people there must have wondered at the fact that the second daughter of Henry VIII had lived to become Queen at twenty-five years of age. Few people could have realized that they were witnessing the beginning of one of the greatest reigns in history.

IMPORTANT DATES

1509	Henry VIII becomes King of England.
	Henry VIII marries Catherine of Aragon.
1516	Mary Tudor is born.
1533	Henry marries Anne Boleyn.
	Henry and Catherine's marriage is declared non-existent.
	Elizabeth is born.
1534	**Act of Parliament** agrees that Henry is Supreme Head of the Church of England.

Elizabeth I wearing her crown.

24

Elizabeth I was to face and overcome many threats and dangers and, finally, to die in 1603 a much-loved and respected monarch. However, when she became Queen in 1558, she had great problems to deal with – little money, religious disagreements, her rival Mary Queen of Scots, the threat of foreign attacks and her need to prove that she could rule England at a time when men gave the orders and women were expected to obey them. Elizabeth was fortunate. She was intelligent and learnt quickly. Above all, her early life had been hard and had taught her how to survive.

Elizabeth appearing in front of her people before her coronation.

Elizabeth's champion, Sir Edward Dymoke, who was prepared to fight anyone who refused to accept her as Queen.

Term 1 | **Unit 5**

IMPORTANT DATES

1536	Anne Boleyn is executed.
	Henry marries Jane Seymour.
1537	Edward is born.
1540	Henry marries Anne of Cleves and, later that year, has the marriage **annulled**.
	Henry marries Catherine Howard.
1542	Catherine Howard is executed.
1543	Henry marries Catherine Parr.
1547	Henry VIII dies and Edward VI becomes King.

Everyone hoped that Elizabeth would be born a boy. **Astrologers** told her parents, Henry VIII and Anne Boleyn, to expect a prince. Elizabeth's birth on 7 September 1533 was a great disappointment. Henry already had a daughter, Mary, by his first wife Catherine of Aragon. Catherine was unable to have more children. Henry needed a son, for he was afraid that if a woman ruled after him, a male rival might try to take the throne from her. Against the Pope's wishes, Henry married Anne Boleyn and then had his marriage to Catherine declared non-existent. Although Henry kept Catholic worship, he became Supreme Head of the Church in England instead of the Pope.

Anne Boleyn, Elizabeth's mother. This picture is a copy of a drawing by Holbein, a German artist who was court painter to Henry VIII.

Henry VIII, Elizabeth's father, at about the time when he fell in love with Anne Boleyn, in around 1526.

The Old Palace, Hatfield House, where Elizabeth stayed as a child.

Henry treated his new daughter well at first, hoping that Anne's next child would be a boy. Although Elizabeth was brought up away from court, she was given much care and attention. Her mother made sure that she was dressed in fashionable clothes made of richly embroidered materials. Unfortunately, Anne **miscarried** the male child Henry wanted so much. She was not given another chance. Accused of having affairs with other men, she was **executed** on 19 May 1536, when Elizabeth was only two and a half years old. Elizabeth was declared **illegitimate** by an Act of Parliament. Her future was not at all certain.

Term 1 | Unit 5

Elizabeth in Danger

At first, the young King was controlled by his uncle, Edward Seymour. Seymour's brother Thomas was jealous, and he planned to marry Elizabeth to gain power for himself. Thomas was arrested, and Elizabeth was also in great danger if the Council could prove that she had agreed to his plans. She convinced her questioners that she had never intended to marry him. Thomas was executed, but Elizabeth was allowed to live.

After Henry VIII's **Reformation**, English rulers could establish whatever religion they chose, and English people had to accept that faith. King Edward VI set up a Protestant Church in England.

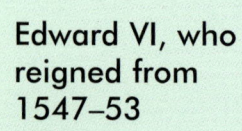

IMPORTANT DATES

1549   Thomas Seymour is sent to the Tower of London.

Seymour is executed.

1553   Edward VI dies.

Lady Jane Grey is proclaimed Queen.

Mary Tudor becomes Queen Mary I.

1554   Lady Jane Grey is executed.

Edward VI, who reigned from 1547–53

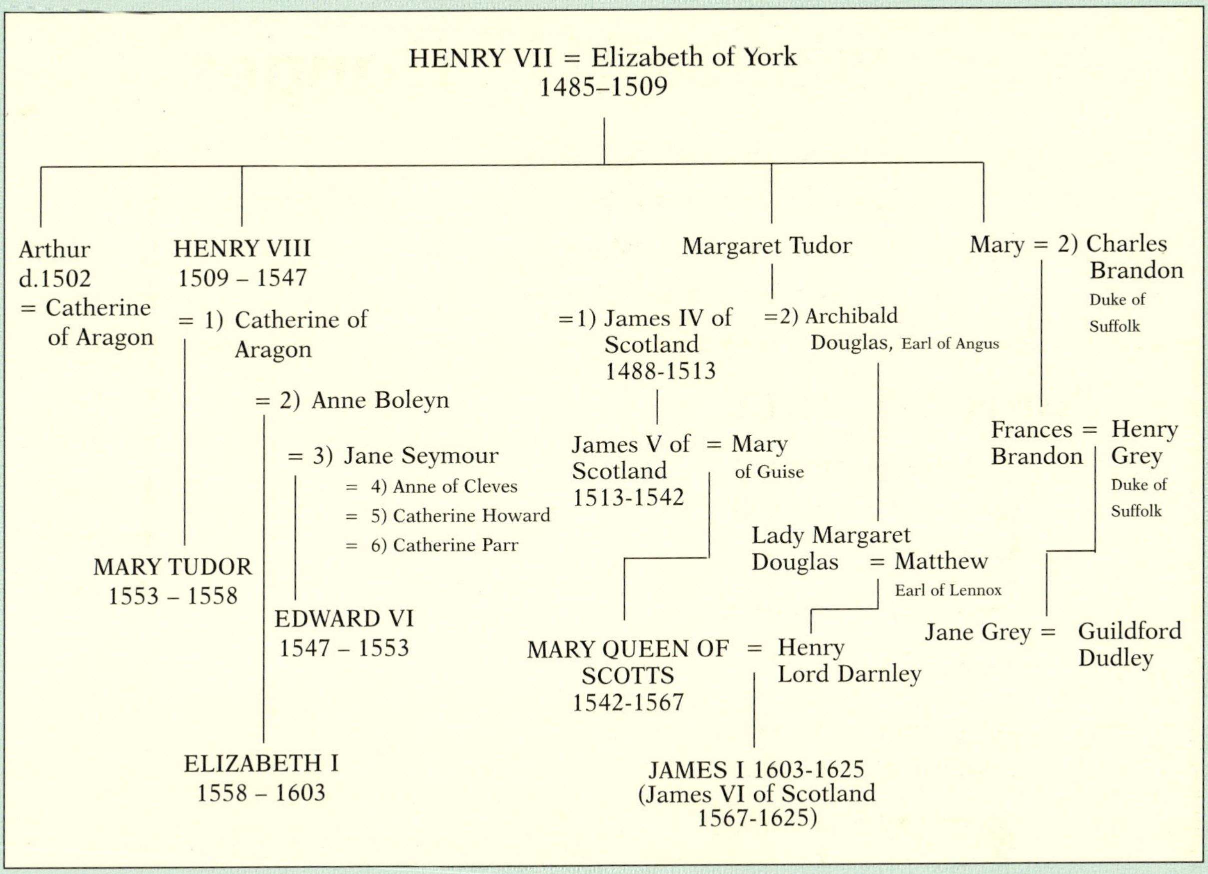

```
                    HENRY VII = Elizabeth of York
                            1485–1509
```

Family tree:

- Arthur d.1502 = Catherine of Aragon
- HENRY VIII 1509 – 1547
  - = 1) Catherine of Aragon
    - MARY TUDOR 1553 – 1558
  - = 2) Anne Boleyn
    - ELIZABETH I 1558 – 1603
  - = 3) Jane Seymour
    - EDWARD VI 1547 – 1553
  - = 4) Anne of Cleves
  - = 5) Catherine Howard
  - = 6) Catherine Parr
- Margaret Tudor
  - =1) James IV of Scotland 1488-1513
    - James V of Scotland 1513-1542 = Mary of Guise
      - MARY QUEEN OF SCOTTS 1542-1567 = Henry Lord Darnley
        - JAMES I 1603-1625 (James VI of Scotland 1567-1625)
  - =2) Archibald Douglas, Earl of Angus
    - Lady Margaret Douglas = Matthew Earl of Lennox
- Mary = 2) Charles Brandon Duke of Suffolk
  - Frances Brandon = Henry Grey Duke of Suffolk
    - Jane Grey = Guildford Dudley

Mary Tudor would be Queen next if Edward died childless, and Mary was determined to restore the **Roman Catholic** religion in England. When Edward died young, his chief adviser, the Duke of Northumberland, tried to prevent this and to keep power for himself. He made his Protestant daughter-in-law, Lady Jane Grey, Queen. Elizabeth remained out of the way until she heard that her sister Mary was advancing on London. Jane, Queen for only nine days, was imprisoned and later executed. Elizabeth went to welcome Mary as Queen.

Elizabeth was next in line to the throne, and she knew that if she became in any way involved in similar plots against Mary, her life would also be in danger.

The family tree of the kings and queens of England and Scotland. It shows the dates of their reigns and how Lady Jane Grey was linked to the royal family.

Term 1 | Unit 5

Mary Tudor aged twenty-eight, before she became Queen.

Mary was determined to make England a Roman Catholic country again. She forced Elizabeth to attend Roman Catholic services, but suspected that Elizabeth remained a Protestant at heart. This angered Mary, for Elizabeth would undo all Mary's religious changes if she became Queen.

When Mary decided to marry King Philip II of Spain, many people were horrified. They hated the idea of England being part of Spain's empire. In desperation, Sir Thomas Wyatt and others tried to overthrow Mary and put Elizabeth on the throne.

The rebellion failed, and Elizabeth was sent to the Tower of London. She went protesting her innocence to her escort. Over the next few weeks she waited for the order for her execution, but it never came. Wyatt was executed, but there was no proof that Elizabeth had become involved. Finally, Elizabeth was released.

Mary never had a child, although at least twice she thought she was pregnant. She burnt almost 300 Protestants trying to persuade people to accept the Roman Catholic faith but, as she lay dying, she knew that she had failed. Her Protestant sister had succeeded her.

Important Dates

1554   Wyatt's rebellion.

Elizabeth is imprisoned briefly in the Tower of London.

Sir Thomas Wyatt is executed.

Mary marries King Philip II of Spain.

1555   Beginning of the burning of Protestants.

Queen Elizabeth's arrest.

Term 1 | Unit 5

Queen at Last

Elizabeth was at Hatfield when she heard that Mary had died. She was twenty-five years old and was convinced that God had chosen her to be Queen. She said, "This is the doing of the Lord; and it is marvellous in our eyes". Although women were expected to take second place to men, Elizabeth always made it clear that she was the ruler of England. She listened to advice, but she alone took the decisions. She loved power. Years of living with an uncertain future had made her careful and wise.

IMPORTANT DATES

1558 — Elizabeth becomes Queen Elizabeth I of England.

1559 — Elizabeth I is crowned Queen of England.

Elizabeth sets up a Protestant Church in England, with herself as Supreme Governor.

1560 — Amy Robsart, Robert Dudley's wife, is found dead.

1579 — Francis, Duke of Alençon, secretly comes to England for the first time, to try and marry Elizabeth.

1581–82 — The Duke of Alençon returns to England.

Elizabeth sits alone while her counsellors stand respectfully to one side.

Elizabeth recognized that she had a great responsibility to her people and she loved them. Most people adored and trusted her. Wherever she went, they cheered her and she would speak to even the humblest of her subjects.

Elizabeth had many problems to face. The country was divided over the question of religion. Mary's attempts to restore England to the Roman Catholic faith had left much bitterness. Protestants quarrelled over what sort of church they wanted Elizabeth to set up. England was a small, weak country compared to the powers of Spain and France. There was always the danger of foreign attacks. There was also the threat of Mary Queen of Scots, who might try to take the English throne. Finally, there was the question of Elizabeth's marriage. Who was she to marry, and when?

Elizabeth's signature. "R" stands for regina, which is Latin for "queen".

Nonsuch Palace, one of Elizabeth's houses. This is the house she is supposed to have liked best.

Term 1 | Unit 5

Triumphs and Troubles

Elizabeth I admired and rewarded people who had the courage to risk their lives and fortunes in exploring the world. She sometimes **invested** in their **expeditions**, because she liked the idea that such adventures weakened the power of the Spanish King, Philip II, who had a great empire. She also expected a share in their profits. Francis Drake, an explorer, made a great voyage round the world in his ship **The Golden Hind** in 1577–80. He brought back treasure and jewels taken from Spanish ships. Elizabeth was given a large amount of the wealth, and she had him knighted.

Drake's cup which celebrates Drake's round-the-world voyage. The model of the world opens on a hinge.

Ceremonies and processions were an important part of court life.

At home, Elizabeth enjoyed going on **progress** in the summer when she would travel round the country with her court, allowing herself to be seen by her people and being entertained. In London or on progress, she was always surrounded by her advisers and those who hoped for favour and promotion, and by her ladies-in-waiting who looked after her comfort. Elizabeth frequently watched plays, and William Shakespeare's **Twelfth Night** was performed at court in 1601. She loved dancing and music, and also liked hunting, **bear-baiting** and watching tournaments. Poets called her "Gloriana" and she encouraged the idea that she was special. This set her apart and made her more powerful.

Elizabeth I travelling round the country. The winged figure of Fame shows how well known she was. Notice how she travels in an open carriage so everyone can see her.

Important Dates

1568	Mary Queen of Scots flees to England.
1570	Pope excommunicates Elizabeth, releasing all English Roman Catholics from their loyalty to her.
1577-80	Francis Drake sails round the world in *The Golden Hind*.
1587	Mary Queen of Scots is executed at Fotheringhay Castle.
1588	Defeat of the Spanish Armada.

Glossary

Act of Parliament A law which is passed in Parliament.

annulled Cancelled, or made invalid.

astrologers People who claim to be able to tell the future by studying the stars.

bear-baiting Bears fighting dogs for sport.

coronation The church service when someone is crowned king or queen.

correspondence Written communications.

executed When someone has been killed as a punishment.

expeditions Long journeys.

illegitimate Someone whose parents were not married when he or she was born.

invest To support a scheme in the hope of gaining something in return. Queen Elizabeth I sometimes invested ships in overseas expeditions.

legitimate Someone whose parents were married when he or she was born.

litter A couch on which a person was carried.

lute A musical instrument like a guitar.

minister The name given to an adviser to the Queen, who had a special government job to do.

miscarried Gave birth to a child too early so it was born dead.

moderate Not extreme.

nosegays Small bunches of flowers which could be held in the hand and smelt.

Privy Council A group of important men who advised the Queen.

progress The official name of Elizabeth's summer tours.

Protestant A Christian person who does not accept the Pope as the Head of the Christian Church.

Puritans Members of the Church of England who wanted to make it less like the Roman Catholic Church.

Reformation A move to change the Catholic Church which reduced the Pope's power.

reluctant Not willing to do something.

Renaissance A time of new ideas in art and learning which had their origins in the study of classical learning.

Roman Catholic Someone who believes the Pope is the Head of the Christian Church, and who obeys the Pope's religious laws.

Secretary of State The King or Queen's most important adviser and minister.

torture To make someone feel great pain.

traitor A person who betrays his or her country to an enemy.

treason Plotting against the King or Queen.

virginals A musical instrument with a keyboard – a little like a small piano.

Leave Me Alone

by David Williams

At home

(The doorbell rings. Mrs Patel opens the door.)

Kate	Hello, Mrs Patel. Is Rani in?
Mrs Patel	No. She went out. I thought she must be with you.
Kate	I haven't seen her.
Mrs Patel	Come in. I want to talk to you. You sit with Rani at school, don't you?
Kate	Yes.
Mrs Patel	How is she doing at school? Is she working hard?
Kate	Well . . .
Mrs Patel	Is Mrs Burns happy with her?
Kate	She likes Rani a lot.
Mrs Patel	My girl has always been good at school. She learned to read very quickly.
Kate	She's very good.
Mrs Patel	But now I have a note from Mrs Burns. She wants to see me about Rani. Do you know why?
Kate	No, Mrs Patel.

Mrs Patel	I told Rani what was in the note. But she didn't want to talk about it. She went out.
Kate	I'll go and look for her.
Mrs Patel	Wait. I want you to tell me. Has Rani been buying a lot of sweets lately? Or other things?
Kate	No. Why?
Mrs Patel	She's such a good girl. But something is wrong just now. Kate, you are her best friend, aren't you?
Kate	Yes, I think so.
Mrs Patel	And you would tell me if something was wrong?
Kate	Well, yes.
Mrs Patel	I want to tell you something. Some money is missing from my purse.
Kate	Have you lost it?
Mrs Patel	I think maybe Rani took it.

Kate	She wouldn't do that!
Mrs Patel	She has never done anything like this before. But I think it is her. It has happened twice now.
Kate	Have you asked Rani?
Mrs Patel	She won't let me talk to her just now. What is wrong with her?
Kate	I don't know.
Mrs Patel	Please talk to her for me. Tell her it doesn't matter about the money. But I want her to talk to me.
Kate	Yes, Mrs Patel. I'll go and find her.

In the street

(It is raining. Rani is standing in a dark corner.)

Kate	Is that you, Rani?
Rani	Leave me alone.

Kate   What are you doing here? Your mum wants you.

Rani   I don't want to see her. I'm going to be in trouble.

Kate   No. She told me . . .

Rani   Look. There's Meg and Sharon. Hide.

Kate   Why?

Rani   I'm scared of them. They won't leave me alone.

Meg   There she is.

Sharon Come here, you.

Kate   Go away. She doesn't want to play.

Sharon We wouldn't play with *her*.

Kate   Why do you want her, then?

Meg   She owes us some money.

Kate   She doesn't.

41

Term 1 | **Unit 7**

Sharon	Shut up.
Meg	Have you got the money?
Rani	It's here. That's all I can get.
Meg	You'll have to get more tomorrow.
Sharon	And you, what's your name?
Kate	Kate.
Sharon	You'd better shut up about it or you'll get this.
	(She shows her fist.)
	Right?
Meg	Come on, Sharon. I'm getting wet.
	(Meg and Sharon leave.)
Kate	You'll have to tell your mum about this.
Rani	I'm scared to. They'll get me if I do. You *must* keep it a secret. Do you promise?
Kate	Will you go back home if I do?
Rani	Yes.
Kate	I promise.

In school

(Kate knocks on the classroom door.)

Mrs Burns	Come in. Hello, Kate. You're early.
Kate	Mrs Burns, can I talk to you?

42

Mrs Burns	Of course.
Kate	Rani is my best friend.
Mrs Burns	I know.
Kate	And I promised her I would keep a secret.
Mrs Burns	Is it the secret that is making her unhappy?
Kate	Yes.
Mrs Burns	If you're her best friend you should tell someone who can help.
Kate	Even if I've promised not to?
Mrs Burns	You should do what you think is right.
Kate	I think it's right to tell.
Mrs Burns	Do you want to tell me?
Kate	Yes. Rani is scared.
Mrs Burns	What of?
Kate	Two big girls. Meg and Sharon.

Term 1 **Unit 7**

Mrs Burns I know them.

Kate They are making Rani give them money.

Mrs Burns What money?

Kate Her mum's. Rani is taking it for the girls. If she won't, they're going to hit her.

Mrs Burns I see. Is she scared to tell her mum?

Kate Yes.

Mrs Burns You were right to tell me, Kate. No one should keep bad secrets.

Kate I'm scared of the girls too.

Mrs Burns Don't worry. Nothing will happen to you or Rani. I promise.

In the playground

Rani Kate.

Kate Hello, Rani.

Rani My mum went to see Mrs Burns. She knows about Meg and Sharon.

44

Kate   Is it all right?

Rani   Yes. They've given Mum all her money back. I saw them too.

Kate   Were you scared?

Rani   No. They cried and they said they were really sorry. They won't harm us any more.

Kate   Rani, *I* told Mrs Burns about them. I broke my promise.

Rani   It doesn't matter. I'm glad you did.

Kate   It's nice to see you smile again.

Rani   It feels nice.

Kate   Come on. Let's show Mrs Burns.

Rani   I'll race you.

Kate   No. Let's go in together.

Rani   Okay.

(They run off, hand in hand)

A Green Harvest

by Wes Magee

A play with five characters

Farmer

Shopkeeper

Gardener

Boy

Girl

– and a Chorus

Chorus As you can see
the Harvest's here,
all gathered in
for one more year.

Ripe, juicy fruits
and golden grain,
it's harvest time
come round again.

But wait, what's this?
Latecomers! See!
Last minute gifts.
Come on, you three!

Farmer Phew, just made it, just in time. Here's a marrow from my farm. I'm the *best* farmer in the district, you know.

Chorus *That* farmer! Best?
You should see his dirty vest!

Gardener I'm not too late am I? Oh, good. Now, here's my contribution to the Harvest Festival. One rather massive pumpkin from my garden. You'll not see a better one. I'm a *grand* gardener, you know.

Chorus *That* gardener! Grand?
Ugh, just look at
his filthy hand!

Shopkeeper Phew, got here. Wow, what a rush. Thought I'd missed the Harvest Festival. Now, this cabbage is from my shop. Wonderful greengrocer's shop I've got. Oh, wonderful. Yes, I'm one *smart* shopkeeper.

Chorus *That* shopkeeper! Smart?
He's got brains,
but not much heart!

Term 1 Unit 8

Farmer	Hey, why are you saying such nasty things about us?
Gardener	Yes, why are you insulting us?
Shopkeeper	We've brought food for your Harvest Festival. You should be jolly grateful.
Chorus	Oh, we are, we are, we're grateful, you know. But just think what happened an hour ago.
Farmer	Happened?
Gardener	An hour ago?
Shopkeeper	Nothing happened. Come on, they're talking nonsense . . . and it's rhyming nonsense, which is even worse!
Chorus	Wait a minute, have no fear. A flashback will make all clear.
Farmer **Gardener** **Shopkeeper**	Flashback?

Chorus   Flashback!!

(Flashback effect.)

Chorus   We're back one hour.
Now look, and see
what you were up to.
One! Two! Three!

Farmer   Now the harvest's gathered in I've got bags of left-over fertilizer. Got to get rid of it somewhere. But where? I know, I'll chuck it *in the river!* Here goes.

Gardener   I've got tons of rotting rubbish from my garden. Phew, it's vile. Where can I dump it? Ah, *the river* will wash it all away. Here goes!

Shopkeeper   I've got piles of junk in my shop. Wooden boxes, cardboard boxes, plastic bags. I'll just dump them here on the *river bank!* No problem. Here goes!

Chorus	Look at these three, dumping their junk. They chuck it away and do a bunk!

(Farmer, Gardener and Shopkeeper try to run away.)

Chorus	Hold it! Stop! STOP!
Farmer	Stop?
Gardener	Us?
Shopkeeper	What for?
Chorus	Dumping rubbish! Polluting the river! Just you listen to this.

(Enter boy and girl.)

Boy   Hey, look at the river. Look at that awful rubbish floating in the water.

Girl   Look, dead fish. All the chemicals and rubbish must have killed them.

Boy   And here's a dead bird.

Girl   This is terrible. The river's ruined, ruined.

Chorus   *(Pointing to Farmer, Gardener and Shopkeeper)*

See what you've done,
You rotten meanies.
We'll have to call in
the clean-up Greenies!

Term 1 | Unit 9

Anne Frank

by Wayne Jackson

Early childhood in Germany

Anne Frank was born on 12 June 1929 in Frankfurt, Germany. She came from a Jewish family who had lived there for hundreds of years. Anne's parents were called Otto and Edith. Her father worked in a bank. The Franks' three-year-old daughter, Margot, was very pleased when Anne was born. She was glad to have a little sister to play with.

Anne's father was a very keen photographer. He took dozens of photos of Anne and Margot as they played in the street or visited their grandparents.

In Germany Jewish people were sometimes treated very unfairly. This is called **anti-Semitism**. But in Frankfurt, anti-Semitism was not as bad as in other parts of Germany. Although Anne's family was not rich, her life was happy and fun.

Anne with her father and sister, Margot (left).

Hitler comes to power

Hitler told Germans not to buy anything from Jewish shopkeepers, and Jews were not allowed to work for the government. Anne could not go to nursery school because she was a "non-**Aryan**". Otto Frank saw that things were getting bad for Jews, so he moved his family to Amsterdam in the Netherlands.

52

Going into hiding

In 1942, two years after the Germans invaded, Anne's grandmother died. Anne was very sad, but her thirteenth birthday cheered her up. Anne's favourite present was a wonderful notebook, which she decided to use as a diary. Anne's diary was to become her best friend, and she called it Kitty.

Only three weeks later the family received a bad shock. Margot was ordered to report for work at a German **labour camp**. The Franks knew what this meant. Margot, because she was Jewish, would be sent to a **concentration camp** where she would almost certainly be killed.

Term 1 | Unit 9

The office building where Anne's father worked, as it is today.

Many Jews were put to death by poisonous gas in concentration camps. Today, we call these terrible killings **the Holocaust**.

That night Otto Frank decided that the whole family must hide away in the secret place he had been preparing for months. They could take only a few things with them because they might have been stopped by the police if they carried suitcases. Anne took her hair curlers, school books, some old letters, a comb and, of course, her diary. She knew they were crazy things to take, but she said, "I'm not sorry; memories mean more to me than dresses."

The Franks hid in secret rooms at the back of the office building.

54

Date chart

1929   Anne Frank born on 12 June in Frankfurt, Germany.

1933   Hitler comes to power in Germany.

1933   Anne Frank's family moves to Amsterdam in the Netherlands.

1939   **Second World War** begins.

1940   The German army invades and occupies the Netherlands.

1940   Anne Frank's family tries and fails to move to England.

1941   Many unfair laws passed against Jewish people in the Netherlands.

1942   Anne is given a diary as a present on her thirteenth birthday. Anne and her family go into hiding in the secret **annexe**.

1944   6 June. The **Allied armies** land in France and begin the liberation of countries occupied by the Germans.

1944   4 August. Someone reveals the Franks' hiding place. All the people living in the annexe are arrested and sent away to concentration camps.

1945   March. Anne Frank and her sister Margot die of typhus in Belsen camp.

1945   8 May. The German army surrenders. The war is over.

1947   Anne Frank's diary is published. More than 20 million copies have been sold.

The **Nazi** symbol was a swastika – the bent cross on the men's armbands.

Glossary

Allied armies The armies from forty-nine countries that fought against Hitler and the Nazis during the Second World War.

Annexe A building attached to a larger building.

Anti-Semitism Treating Jewish people unfairly, just because they are Jewish.

Aryan A race of people believed by the Nazis to be the best in the world. Aryans were non-Jewish Europeans.

Betray To reveal or give up a person to an enemy.

Concentration camps Special prisons set up by the Nazis for certain types of people that Hitler thought inferior, such as Jews, gypsies and blacks. Many people died in concentration camps.

Hitler The leader of Germany from 1933 to 1945 and head of the Nazi party. Hitler blamed Germany's problems on the Jews, and he tried to get rid of all Jews in Europe.

The Holocaust The mass murder of the Jews by the Nazis during the Second World War. About six million Jews were killed.

Inferior Of less worth.

Labour camp A place where prisoners had to work for the Nazis.

Nazis Members of Adolf Hitler's National Socialist German Workers' Party.

Refugees People who move from their own country to seek safety in another country.

Second World War The fighting that broke out in many parts of the world between 1939 and 1945. It started when Germany invaded Poland and involved many countries.

Typhus A serious illness caused by a poor diet and filthy conditions.

Books to read

For older readers:

Anne Frank Journal (Anne Frank Foundation, Amsterdam, 1988)

The Diary of Anne Frank by Anne Frank (Pan Books, 1982)

Eva's Story (A Step-sister's Story) by Eva Schloss (W.H. Allen, 1988)

Tales from the House Behind by Anne Frank (Piccolo, 1971)

For younger readers:

Anne Frank by Angela Bull (Hamish Hamilton, 1984)

Anne Frank by Vanora Leigh (Wayland, 1985)

Anne Frank by Richard Tames (Franklin Watts, 1989)

For further information:
The Anne Frank Educational Trust, PO Box 11880, London N6 4LN. Tel: 0181 340 9077

When Hitler Stole Pink Rabbit *by Judith Kerr*

Chapter Two

Anna's first thought was so terrible that she could not breathe. Papa had got worse in the night. He had been taken to hospital. Perhaps he . . . She ran blindly out of the room and found herself caught by Heimpi.

"It's all right!" said Heimpi. "It's all right! Your father has gone on a journey."

"A journey?" Anna could not believe it. "But he's ill – he had a temperature . . ."

"He decided to go just the same," said Heimpi firmly. "Your mother was going to explain it all to you when you came home from school. Now I suppose you'll have to hear straight away and Fräulein Schmidt will be kept twiddling her thumbs for you."

"What is it? Are we going to miss school?" Max appeared hopefully on the landing.

Then Mama came out of her room. She was still in her dressing-gown and looked tired.

"There's no need to get terribly excited," she said. "But there are some things I must tell you. Heimpi, shall we have some coffee? And I expect the children could eat some more breakfast."

Once they were all settled in Heimpi's pantry with coffee and rolls Anna felt much better, and was even able to calculate that she would miss the geography lesson at school which she particularly disliked.

"It's quite simple," said Mama. "Papa thinks Hitler and the Nazis might win the elections. If that happened he would not want to live in Germany while they were in power, and nor would any of us."

"Because we're Jews?" asked Anna.

"Not only because we're Jews. Papa thinks no one would be allowed to say what they thought any more, and he wouldn't be able to write. The Nazis don't like people to disagree with them." Mama drank some of her coffee and looked more cheerful. "Of course it may never happen and if it did it probably wouldn't last for long – maybe six months or so. But at the moment we just don't know."

"But why did Papa leave so suddenly?" asked Max.

"Because yesterday someone rang him up and warned him that they might be going to take away his passport. So I packed him a small suitcase and he caught the night train to Prague – that's the quickest way out of Germany."

"Who could take away his passport?"

"The police. There are quite a few Nazis in the police."

"And who rang him up to warn him?"

Mama smiled for the first time.

"Another policeman. One Papa had never met – but who had read his books and liked them."

It took Anna and Max some time to digest all this.

Then Max asked, "But what's going to happen now?"

"Well," said Mama, "it's only about ten days until the elections. Either the Nazis lose, in which case Papa comes back – or they win, in which case we join him."

"In Prague?" asked Max.

"No, probably in Switzerland. They speak German there – Papa would be able to write. We'd probably rent a little house and stay there until all this has blown over."

"Heimpi too?" asked Anna.

"Heimpi too."

It sounded quite exciting. Anna was beginning to imagine it – a house in the mountains . . . goats . . . or was it cows? . . . when Mama said, "There is one thing more." Her voice was very serious.

"This is the most important thing of all," said Mama, "and we need you to help us with it. Papa does not want anyone to know that he has left Germany. So you must not tell anyone. If anyone asks you about him you must say that he's still in bed with flu."

"Can't I even tell Gunther?" asked Max.

"No. Not Gunther, nor Elsbeth, not anyone."

"All right," said Max. "But it won't be easy. People are always asking after him."

"Why can't we tell anyone?" asked Anna. "Why doesn't Papa want anyone to know?"

"Look," said Mama. "I've explained it all to you as well as I can. But you're both still children – you can't understand everything. Papa thinks the Nazis might . . . cause us some bother if they knew that he'd gone. So he does not want you to talk about it. Now are you going to do what he asks or not?"

Anna said, yes, of course she would.

Then Heimpi bundled them both off to school. Anna was worried about what to say if anyone asked her why she was late, but Max said, "Just tell them Mama overslept – she did, anyway!"

In fact, no one was very interested. They did high-jump in Gym and Anna jumped higher than anyone else in her class. She was so pleased about this that for the rest of the morning she almost forgot about Papa being in Prague.

When it was time to go home it all came back to her and she hoped Elsbeth would not ask her any awkward questions – but Elsbeth's mind was on more important matters. Her aunt was coming to take her out that afternoon to buy her a yo-yo. What kind did Anna think she should choose? And what colour? The wooden ones worked best on the whole, but Elsbeth had seen a bright orange one which, though made of tin, had so impressed her with its beauty that she was tempted. Anna only had to say Yes and No, and by the time she got home for lunch the day felt more ordinary than she would ever have thought possible that morning.

Neither Anna nor Max had any homework and it was too cold to go out, so in the afternoon they sat on the radiator in the nursery and looked out of the window. The wind was rattling the shutters and blowing great lumps of cloud across the sky.

"We might get more snow," said Max.

"Max," said Anna, "do you hope that we will go to Switzerland?"

"I don't know," said Max. There were so many things he would miss. Gunther . . . his gang with whom he played football . . . school . . . He said, "I suppose we'd go to a school in Switzerland."

"Oh yes," said Anna. "I think it would be quite fun." She was almost ashamed to admit it, but the more she thought about it the more she wanted to go. To be in a strange country where everything would be different – to live in a different house, go to a different school with different children – a huge urge to experience it all overcame her and though she knew it was heartless a smile appeared on her face.

"It would only be for six months," she said apologetically, "and we'd all be together."

The next few days passed fairly normally. Mama got a letter from Papa. He was comfortably installed in a hotel in Prague and was feeling much better. This cheered everyone up.

A few people inquired after him but were quite satisfied

when the children said he had 'flu. There was so much of it about that it was not surprising. The weather continued very cold and the puddles caused by the thaw all froze hard again – but still there was no snow.

At last on the afternoon of the Sunday before the elections the sky turned very dark and then suddenly opened up to release a mass of floating, drifting, whirling white. Anna and Max were playing with the Kentner children who lived across the road. They stopped to watch the snow come down.

"If only it had started a bit earlier," said Max. "By the time it's thick enough for tobogganing, it will be too dark."

At five o'clock when Anna and Max were going home it had only just stopped. Peter and Marianne Kentner saw them to the door. The snow lay thick and dry and crunchy all over the road and the moon was shining down on it.

"Why don't we go tobogganing in the moonlight?" said Peter.

"Do you think they'd let us?"

"We've done it before," said Peter, who was fourteen. "Go and ask your mother."

Mama said they could go provided they all stayed together and got home by seven. They put on their warmest clothes and set off.

It was only a quarter of an hour's walk to the Grunewald, where a wooden slope made an ideal run down to a frozen lake. They had tobogganed there many times before, but it had always been daylight and the air had been loud with the shouts of other children. Now all they could hear was the soughing of the wind in the trees, the crunching of the new snow under their feet, and the gentle whir of the sledges as they slid along behind them. Above their heads the sky was dark but the ground shone blue in the moonlight and the shadows of the trees broke like black bands across it.

At the top of the slope they stopped and looked down. Nobody had been on it before them. The shimmering path of snow stretched ahead, perfect and unmarked, right down to the edge of the lake.

"Who's going down first?" asked Max.

Anna did not mean to, but she found herself hopping up and down and saying. "Oh please – please . . . !"

Peter said, "All right – youngest first."

That meant her because Marianne was ten.

She sat on her sledge, held on to the steering rope, took a deep breath and pushed off. The sledge began to move, rather gently, down the hill.

"Go on!" shouted the boys behind her. "Give it another push!"

But she didn't. She kept her feet on the runners and let the sledge gather speed slowly. The powdery snow sprayed up all round her as the sledge struck it. The trees moved past, slowly at first, then faster and faster. The moonlight leapt all round her. At last she seemed to be flying through a mass of silver. Then the sledge hit the hump at the bottom of the slope, shot across it, and landed in a dapple of moonlight on the frozen lake. It was beautiful.

The others came down after her, squealing and shouting.

They went down the slope head first on their stomachs so that the snow sprayed straight into their faces. They went down feet first on their backs with the black tops of the fir trees rushing past above them. They all squeezed on to one sledge together and came down so fast that they shot on almost to the middle of the lake. After each ride they struggled back up the slope, panting and pulling the sledges behind them. In spite of the cold they were steaming inside their woollies.

Then it began to snow again. At first they hardly noticed it, but then the wind got up and blew the snow in their faces. All at once Max stopped in the middle of dragging his sledge up the slope and said, "What time is it? Oughtn't we to be getting back?"

Nobody had a watch and they suddenly realized that they had no idea how long they had been there. Perhaps it was quite late and their parents had been waiting for them at home.

"Come on," said Peter. "We'd better go quickly." He took off his gloves and knocked them together to shake the caked snow off them. His hands were red with cold. So were Anna's, and she noticed for the first time that her feet were frozen.

It was chilly going back. The wind blew through their damp clothes and with the moon hidden behind the clouds the path was black in front of them. Anna was glad when they were out of the trees and in a road. Soon there were street lamps, houses with lighted windows, shops. They were nearly home.

An illuminated clockface showed them the time. After all it was not yet quite seven. They heaved sighs of relief and walked more slowly. Max and Peter began to talk about football. Marianne tied two sledges together and scampered wildly ahead on the empty road, leaving a network of overlapping tracks in the snow. Anna lagged behind because her cold feet hurt.

She could see the boys stop outside her house, still talking and waiting for her, and was just going to catch them up when she heard the creak of a gate. Something moved in the path beside her and suddenly a shapeless figure loomed up. For a moment she was very frightened – but then she saw that it was only Fräulein Lambeck in some sort of furry cloak and with a letter in her hand.

"Little Anna!" cried Fräulein Lambeck. "Fancy meeting you in the dark of the night! I was just going to the post box but did not think to find a kindred spirit. And how is your dear Papa?"

"He's got 'flu," said Anna automatically.

Fräulein Lambeck stopped in her tracks.

"Still got 'flu, little Anna? You told me he had 'flu a week ago."

"Yes," said Anna.

"And he's still in bed? Still got a temperature?"

"Yes," said Anna.

"Oh, the poor man!" Fräulein Lambeck put a hand on Anna's shoulder. "Are they doing everything for him? Does the doctor come to see him?"

"Yes," said Anna.

"And what does the doctor say?"

"He says . . . I don't know," said Anna.

Fräulein Lambeck leaned down confidentially and peered into her face. "Tell me, little Anna," she said, "how high is your dear papa's temperature?"

"I don't know!" cried Anna, and her voice came out not at all as she had meant but in a sort of squeak. "I'm sorry but I must go home now!" – and she ran as fast as she could towards Max and the open front door.

"What's the matter with you?" said Heimpi in the hall. "Someone shoot you out of a cannon?"

Anna could see Mama through the half-open door in the drawing room.

"Mama!" she cried, "I hate lying to everybody about Papa. It's horrible. Why do we have to do it? I wish we didn't have to!"

Then she saw that mama was not alone. Onkel Julius (who was not really an uncle but an old friend of Papa's) was sitting in an armchair on the other side of the room.

"Calm yourself," said Mama quite sharply. "We all hate lying about Papa, but just now it's necessary. I wouldn't ask you to do it if it weren't necessary!"

"She got caught by Fräulein Lambeck," said Max who had followed Anna in. "You know Fräulein Lambeck? She's ghastly. You can't answer her questions even when you're allowed to tell the truth!"

"Poor Anna," said Onkel Julius in his high voice. He was a gentle wispy man and they were all very fond of him. "Your father asked me to tell you that he misses you both very much and sends you lots of love."

"Have you seen him then?" asked Anna.

"Onkel Julius has just come back from Prague," said Mama. "Papa is fine, and he wants us to meet him in Zurich, in Switzerland, on Sunday."

"Sunday?" said Max. "But that's only a week. That's the day of the elections. I thought we were going to wait and see who won, first!"

"Your father has decided he'd rather not wait." Onkel Julius smiled at Mama. "I do think he's taking all this too seriously."

"Why?" asked Max. "What's he worried about?"

Mama sighed. "Ever since Papa heard of the move to take away his passport he's been worried that they might try to take away ours – then we wouldn't be able to leave Germany."

"But why should they?" asked Max. "If the Nazis don't like us, surely they'd be glad to get rid of us."

"Exactly," said Onkel Julius. He smiled at Mama again. "Your husband is a wonderful man with a wonderful imagination, but frankly in this matter I think he's off his head. Never mind, you'll all have a lovely holiday in Switzerland and when you come back to Berlin in a few weeks' time we'll all go to the Zoo together." Onkel Julius was a naturalist and went to the Zoo all the time. "Let me know if I can help with any of the arrangements. I'll see you again, of course." He kissed Mama's hand and went.

"Are we really leaving on Sunday?" asked Anna.

"Saturday," said Mama. "It's a long way to Switzerland. We have to spend a night in Stuttgart on the way."

"Then this is our last week at school!" said Max.

It seemed incredible.

Term 1 | Unit 11

Let's Celebrate Winter *by Rhoda Nottridge*

Midwinter Festivals

Midwinter is the time in the year when many parts of the world have daylight for only a short time and the nights are very long.

Years ago, in northern Europe, there were torchlit processions and big bonfires in midwinter. People would find a huge log of wood and put it on the bonfire. This was called the yule log. It burned for three days. Then the people kept some of the ash from the log to give them good luck in the new year.

In northern Europe in ancient times people believed in ghosts. They thought that at their midwinter festival, the ghosts of their dead friends and families visited them. In China and some other countries it is still a time to remember the dead. Chinese families invite the ghosts to a special feast and offer gifts to them to keep them happy.

In Finland, candles are put on family graves in midwinter to remember the dead.

A cake shaped like a wooden log is a part of midwinter celebrations in some countries.

Christmas Customs

At Christmas time there are many traditions which are carried out every year. Some of them have been going on for hundreds of years. Putting a piece of mistletoe up is a custom that began before Christmas was a Christian festival. It comes from a time in Britain when mistletoe was a very important plant to an ancient people called the Druids.

Some customs come from the old midwinter festivals of northern Europe. In ancient stories, a god called Odin visited the earth in midwinter. He rewarded good people and punished bad people. When Christianity spread, Saint Nicholas replaced Odin in the stories. Saint Nicholas brought gifts to good children. In the Netherlands, Saint Nicholas was called Sinterklaas. Nowadays he is called Santa Claus in many parts of the world.

People celebrate Christmas in many parts of the world. This building is decorated for Christmas in Hong Kong.

Every year children send letters to Santa Claus. They hope he will make their wishes come true.

73

Term 1 | Unit 11

Christmas Time

Christmas is a festival which celebrates the birth of Jesus Christ. In many parts of the world, Christians celebrate the 25 December each year. In cold countries Christmas became a part of the old midwinter celebrations. In some countries, such as Australia or South Africa, December is in the middle of the summer so it is warm at Christmas time.

In Sweden there is a special Christian festival on 13 December for Saint Lucia. One girl is chosen to be the Lucia queen, and there is a procession where the girls carry candles and wear long, white dresses.

In ancient times, the Romans had a festival called Saturnalia which they celebrated in December. The Christians chose to celebrate the birth of Christ during Saturnalia. The Romans became Christians and so they started to celebrate the Christmas festival instead of Saturnalia. However, some of the old celebrations were carried on in the new Christian festival. The custom of having parties and decorating homes with holly and ivy goes back to Saturnalia.

During the Roman festival of Saturnalia everyone had a merry time. Some of the old customs became part of the Christian festival of Christmas.

Term 1 | Unit 11

Light the Festive Candles

(For Hanukkah)

Light the first of eight tonight –
the farthest candle to the right.

Light the first and second, too,
when tomorrow's day is through.

Then light three, and then light four –
every dusk one candle more

Till all eight burn bright and high,
honouring a day gone by

When the Temple was restored,
rescued from the Syrian lord,

And an eight-day feast proclaimed –
The Festival of Lights – well named

To celebrate the joyous day
when we regained the right to pray
to our one God in our own way.

Aileen Fisher

The Jewish festival of Hanukkah lasts eight days, and on each day a candle is lit in a special holder called a menorah. The festival celebrates the Syrians being driven out of Jerusalem and the Jews regaining their freedom to worship in the Temple.

Crown of Light Festival

Stars gleaming overhead,
    evening air's clear,
    and Advent is here,
    now in Sweden.

Golden-haired girls
    in each village and town
    wear a white flowing gown,
    now in Sweden.

With a crown of green leaves,
    and candles all bright,
    on St Lucia's night,
    now in Sweden.

Snowflakes are dancing,
    as bells start to ring,
    and the children's choirs sing,
    now in Sweden.

David Bateson

The festival of St Lucia is celebrated all over Sweden on December 13th. A legend says that Lucy took food to Christians in the caves under Rome, wearing lights on her head – hence the five candles in the crown of leaves.

Seymour Finds a Home
by Dyan Sheldon

Chapter One

Once upon a time, in a land very far from here, there was a young dragon whose name was Seymour. In many ways, Seymour was a very average dragon. He was the average size for a young dragon – about the size of a small horse. He was the average colour for a young dragon – green and blue with purple feet and a yellow stomach. And he was the average shape for a young dragon – rather like a pear with small, pointy ears and a long, sharp tail.

Seymour had the average number of toes, and scales, and eyes and nostrils for a young dragon, too.

In fact, if you had put all the young dragons of that very faraway land together in a long line, you would have said that they were all pretty much the same. You would have thought that once you'd seen one dragon you'd more or less seen them all. But you would have been wrong. Seymour was different.

Seymour could roar until the ground shook, just like all the other dragons.

Seymour could belch until his eyes popped, just like all the other dragons.

Seymour could run and play until the sun went down, just like all the other dragons.

And, just like all the other dragons, Seymour could frighten the bravest knight with a flick of his powerful tail.

There was one thing, however, that Seymour couldn't do. He couldn't breathe fire, like all the other dragons could. Not even a very small fire. Not even enough to light a match.

Seymour would huff and puff and growl and roar, but when he opened his mouth he didn't breathe one single spark. Seymour would roll his eyes, and stamp his foot, and thump his tail, but when he opened his mouth all that came out was snow.

Cold, white snow.

If the day was especially warm and sunny, he breathed rain. Clear, wet rain.

And sometimes, if he was in a very bad mood, he breathed tiny tornadoes.

But he never breathed fire and smoke.

Obviously, Seymour had problems.

For one thing, it was very difficult to make beautiful princesses scream by breathing snow showers. It made them chilly and grumpy, but it didn't actually scare them. Sometimes they even found it funny.

"Hahahahaha," they would laugh. "Get a load of the dragon with the snow."

For another thing, knights were not too keen on fighting a dragon who breathed sudden storms. It was damp and cold and it rusted their armour. And most of the time they couldn't fight because they were laughing so hard.

"Hehehehehe," they giggled. "You're not a dragon, you're a spring shower with ears."

But the worst thing of all was that none of the other young dragons wanted to play with Seymour. Not even once in a while. Not even when there was no one else to play with. Not even when they were bored and had nothing to do. Not ever. Not at all.

This wasn't because Seymour wasn't a nice dragon.

This wasn't because Seymour wasn't a friendly dragon.

This wasn't because he cheated at games or because he was a bully.

It was because every time one of the other dragons roared and breathed fire, Seymour roared and put it out. The other dragons didn't find this amusing.

"I can blow a flame that's red, yellow and blue," boasted one young dragon. "It can reach the tops of the trees."

"I can blow a flame that's as wide as a river and as hot as the sun," bragged another.

"And I can melt a mountain with my breath," announced a third.

"But Seymour," they all shouted together, "Seymour can only water the grass."

And then they laughed and laughed and laughed. And went off to play by themselves.

Eskimo Lullaby

It's my fat baby
I feel in my hood,
Oh, how heavy he is!

When I turn my head
He smiles at me, my baby,
Hidden in my hood,
Oh, how heavy he is!

How pretty he is when he smiles
With his two teeth, like a little walrus!
Oh I like my baby heavy
And my hood full!

Anon (Greenland)

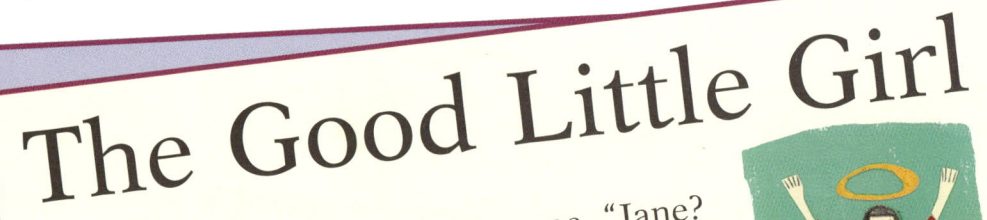

The Good Little Girl

It's funny how often they say to me, "Jane?
    Have you been a *good* girl?"
    "Have you been a *good* girl?"
And when they have said it, they say it again,
    "Have you been a *good* girl?"
    "Have you been a *good* girl?"

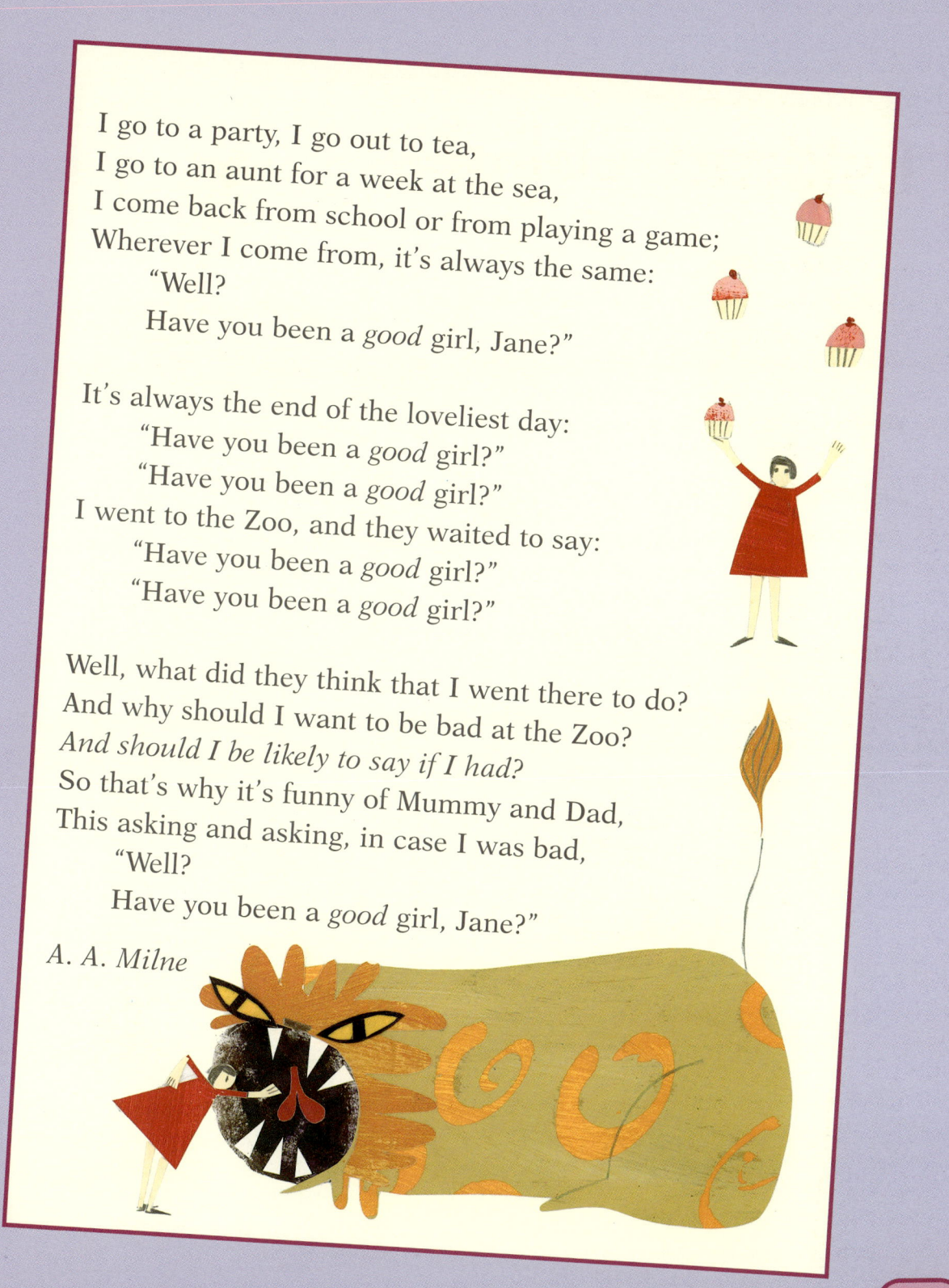

I go to a party, I go out to tea,
I go to an aunt for a week at the sea,
I come back from school or from playing a game;
Wherever I come from, it's always the same:
    "Well?
        Have you been a *good* girl, Jane?"

It's always the end of the loveliest day:
    "Have you been a *good* girl?"
    "Have you been a *good* girl?"
I went to the Zoo, and they waited to say:
    "Have you been a *good* girl?"
    "Have you been a *good* girl?"

Well, what did they think that I went there to do?
And why should I want to be bad at the Zoo?
And should I be likely to say if I had?
So that's why it's funny of Mummy and Dad,
This asking and asking, in case I was bad,
    "Well?
        Have you been a *good* girl, Jane?"

A. A. Milne

Quartermaster's Stores

There were rats, rats
running around in hats
in the stores
in the stores.
There were rats, rats
running around in hats
in the Quartermaster's Stores.

My eyes are dim
I cannot see,
I have not brought my specs with me
I have not brought my specs with me.

There were eggs, eggs
running around on legs
in the stores
in the stores.
There were eggs, eggs
running around on legs
in the Quartermaster's Stores.

My eyes are dim
I cannot see,

I have not brought my specs with me
I have not brought my specs with me.

There was cheese, cheese
crawling on its knees
in the stores
in the stores.
There was cheese, cheese
crawling on its knees
in the Quartermaster's Stores.

My eyes are dim
I cannot see,
I have not brought my specs with me
I have not brought my specs with me.

There was jelly, jelly
sliding on its belly
in the stores
in the stores.
There was jelly, jelly
sliding on its belly
in the Quartermaster's Stores.

My eyes are dim
I cannot see,
I have not brought my specs with me
I have not brought my specs with me.

Anon

Allie

"Allie, call the birds in,
The birds from the sky."
Allie calls, Allie sings,
Down they all fly.

First there came
Two white doves
Then a sparrow from his nest,
Then a clucking bantam hen,
Then a robin red-breast.

"Allie, call the beasts in,
The beasts, every one."
Allie calls, Allie sings,
In they all run.
First there came
Two black lambs,
Then a grunting Berkshire sow,
Then a dog without a tail,
Then a red and white cow.

"Allie, call the fish up,
The fish from the stream."
Allie calls, Allie sings,
Up they all swim.
First there came
Two gold fish,
A minnow and a miller's thumb,

Then a pair of loving trout,
Then the twisted eels come.

"Allie, call the children,
Children from the green."
Allie calls, Allie sings,
Soon they run in.
First there came
Tom and Madge,
Kate and I who'll not
    forget
How we played by the
    water's edge
Till the April sun set.

Robert Graves

My Bonnie

My Bonnie lies over the ocean,
My Bonnie lies over the sea,
My Bonnie lies over the ocean;
Oh bring back my Bonnie to me.

Bring back, Bring back,
Oh bring back my Bonnie to me, to me.
Bring back, Bring back,
Oh bring back my Bonnie to me.

Oh blow ye winds over the ocean,
Oh blow ye winds over the sea,
Oh blow ye winds over the ocean
And bring back my Bonnie to me.

Last night as I lay on my pillow,
Last night as I lay on my bed,
Last night as I lay on my pillow
I dreamed my poor Bonnie was dead.

The winds have blown over the ocean,
The winds have blown over the sea,
The winds have blown over the ocean
And brought back my Bonnie to me.

Anon

Praise Song of the Wind

Trees with weak roots
I will strike, I the wind.
I will roar, I will whistle.

Haycocks built today
I will scatter, I the wind.
I will roar, I will whistle.

Badly made haycocks
I will carry off, I the wind.
I will roar, I will whistle.

Uncovered stacks of sheaves
I will soak through, I the wind.
I will roar, I will whistle.

Houses not tightly roofed
I will destroy, I the wind.
I will roar, I will whistle.

Hay piled in sheds
I will tear apart, I the wind.
I will roar, I will whistle.

Fire kindled in the road
I will set flickering, I the wind.
I will roar, I will whistle.

Houses with bad smoke-holes
I will shake, I the wind.
I will roar, I will whistle.

The farmer who does not think
I will make to think, I the wind.
I will roar, I will whistle.

The worthless slug-a-bed
I will wake, I the wind.
I will roar, I will whistle.

Anon (Teleut People of Siberia)

The Panther Roars

The panther roars on the mountain,
The tiger roars in the forest,
The king roars on his throne
With sword and shield in hand.

Anon (Gond, India)

Spook Spotting

by Mary Hooper

I heard Hannah pounding back upstairs two steps at a time, but I didn't dare stop reading. It was *Spooks and Superghosts* and I was just coming to the good bit – the bit where the massively horrible fiend from the lake enters the abbey and meets the ghost of the long-dead knight on horseback. I'd read it before, of course, so I knew what was going to happen, but it was still really exciting.

Hannah burst into the bedroom. "Guess what!" she said.

Well, I didn't think it was anything much – she'd only gone downstairs to tell her mum that she'd seen a lesser spotted something-or-other flying past. Hannah was a bird-watcher, you see; I ought to mention that straight away.

I rolled my eyes. "Bet it's just that you've seen some daft old bird in the garden," I said.

"No, it's better than that. Put that silly spook book down, Amy, and guess properly."

It was Saturday – the Saturday before half-term week. We were round at Hannah's house and her mum was going to take us to the cinema that afternoon. I wanted to see *Adventure at Craghill Spar* ("A riveting real-life story of how two brave children foil a malicious medieval spirit and return a kingdom to its rightful owner" – I'd already read the book) and Hannah wanted to see some nature film about a bird and a dog walking across a desert.

Grudgingly, keeping my finger on the line I was on, I put my book down and looked up at her. "A golden eagle just swooped down and carried off the cat?"

"Don't be stupid," she said, "you don't get golden eagles round here." She stationed herself back by the window – she'd been there most of the morning. "But I do have to keep looking out, because the wind's blowing from the east and I'm sure we're going to see some sea birds. Maybe a kittiwake will go by. I mean, I know we're some distance from . . ."

I went back to *Spooks and Superghosts*. The only thing that worried me was that the long-departed knight on horseback had to come out of a concealed cupboard place where he'd been boarded up for a couple of hundred years, and in the illustration the cupboard plainly wasn't even big enough for the knight, let alone a horse in full armour.

"Of course, with sea birds . . ." Hannah was saying, and then she stopped. "Amy! You haven't guessed."

"Give up," I mumbled, anxious to get back to the knight.

"Well," she said tantalizingly. "My dad just said he's got to go to Wales on business all next week . . . and if we like he'll take us to stay with my gran and gramps – they live on the way!"

I put down *Spooks and Superghosts*.

"Really?" I said.

"All on our own!" Hannah gloated. "No mums or dads!"

Well, I'd never met Hannah's gran and grandad, but the thought of staying anywhere on our own was exciting. So far, the only place I'd been without Mum was the school's country farm. Great, I'd thought then, freedom – but there had been so many teachers and minders that if you so much as blew your nose three of them asked you if you were coming down with a cold.

"They're all right, Gran and Gramps," said Hannah. "They'll be busy, mind, because it's the last week that the castle's open to the public this season and . . ."

"*Castle!*" I squealed.

"Yes, castle," she said calmly, just as if she was telling me that they had a sub post office. "They don't own it, of course. They're just tenants for the National Trust. Housekeepers."

"But . . . but . . . housekeepers in a *castle*!"

She nodded again. "It's not that big, you know. Old, but not big. A fortified manor house, they call it."

"Oh, wow!" I said, while knights in armour, princesses leaning out of towers, ghosts with their heads under their arms, and dreadful horrid fiends jostled in my head for attention. "But . . . I mean – is it a *real* castle? Is it *haunted*?"

"Haunted?" she said. "I shouldn't think so. Gran wouldn't hold with anything like that."

"But . . . are there vampires in the spare rooms and do you wake in the night to the sound of chains rattling? When you open cupboards do skeletons fall out and will there be priests' holes in the walls? And –"

"Of course not," Hannah said, screwing up her face in disgust. "But what is exciting is that a part of the grounds is kept as a wildlife sanctuary, so there should be some pretty rare birds around. Of course, they won't be nesting at this time of year, but I just bet I see some good ones."

"I bet . . ." I breathed. Before *Spooks and Superghosts*, I'd been reading a book where a girl had gone to a castle, found an old mirror, and through it had travelled back in time. While in the sixteenth century she'd saved a witch's life (only she wasn't really a witch, just an old woman who made potions out of herbs) and been given some treasure in return. She'd left the treasure behind when she'd gone back to the twentieth century, but she'd remembered where she'd hidden it, and found it again in time to save the life of her little brother (Simon, called Sine), who needed a very expensive operation. *A Witch in Time Saves Sine* it was called. Great, it was.

"Er . . . are there any big mirrors in the castle?" I asked Hannah. "Any really old ones which go all misty when you look into them?"

"Don't think so," she said.

I was disappointed, but got over it. "Bet you wouldn't notice a mysterious old mirror anyway, not unless it had a robin perched on it."

"I might not even notice it then," said Hannah. "Robins aren't exactly head turning, are they? I might notice if it was a corn bunting or a long-eared owl."

I giggled, and then I thought, well, there were bound to be some mirrors in the castle – it was just up to me to find the right one. *And* find the priests' holes and half-dead vampires and mysterious, wailing maidens who were there one minute and vanished into mist the next.

"I'm going to discover some spooks!" I said to Hannah. "I'm going to find secret rooms and . . . and walled-up skeletons and ghostly, walking monks." I remembered a programme I'd seen on TV about a girl who was always having spooky things happen to her. "I'm going to be world famous for discovering them. I'm going to be on television!"

"Oh, right," said Hannah. "I take it you want to come, then."

"Try and stop me!" I said.

The Conker as Hard as a Diamond
by Chris Powling

Chapter One

Hello!

This is the story of Little Alpesh and the conker as hard as a diamond. It's rather a *strange* story. To tell you the truth I'm not sure I believe it myself – and I'm telling it. Let's hope you're better at believing things than I am.

Alpesh was a little lad with wide-awake eyes, jet-black hair and a grin on his face so big and friendly that you felt like his best mate the instant you met him. Why was he such a jumpy kid, though? Why did he keep on staring upwards and downwards and from side to side all the time as if he were looking for something?

Well, he was looking for something – something so special nobody in the world had ever found it before. Actually, nobody in the world except Little Alpesh had even thought of *looking* for it before.

What was it?

I've already told you. For weeks and weeks and weeks

now Little Alpesh had been hoping to discover THE CONKER AS HARD AS A DIAMOND.

"Do what?" the other kids said.

"The conker as hard as a diamond," said Little Alpesh, "that's what I'm looking for. It's got to be round here somewhere."

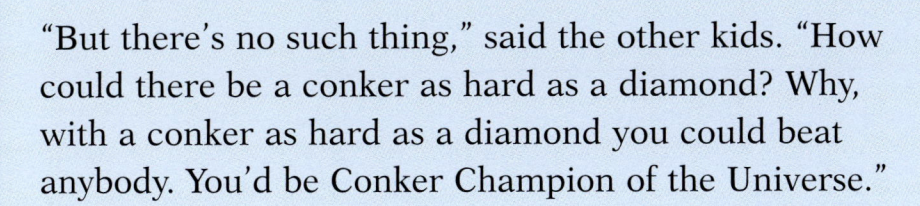

"But there's no such thing," said the other kids. "How could there be a conker as hard as a diamond? Why, with a conker as hard as a diamond you could beat anybody. You'd be Conker Champion of the Universe."

"Exactly," said Little Alpesh.

"You?" said the other kids. "Conker Champion of the Universe? Little Alpesh? Everybody else would have to play with glass conkers for you to be Conker Champion of the Universe. Remember last year?"

"Yes," said Little Alpesh sadly.

"Last year you didn't win a single conker game. Not one."

"I know," said Little Alpesh.

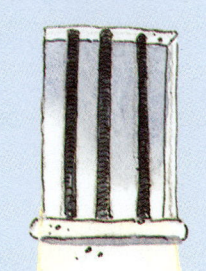

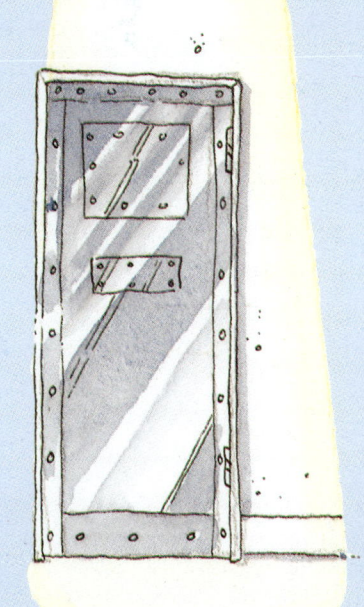

Chapter Four

The conker as hard as a diamond was now in gaol.

Just think of it: four whitewashed walls like a tall bathroom without any bathroom tiles; one high-up window with bars as thick as a tiger's tail; one steel

97

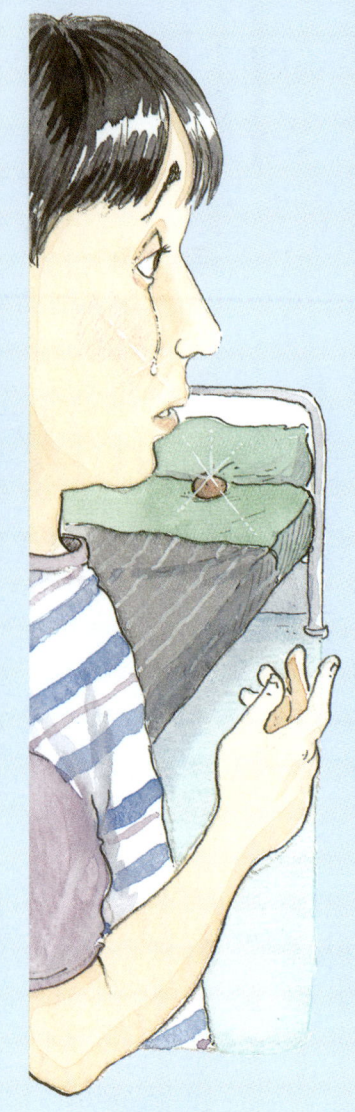

door locked so tight not even a burglar the size of a flea could get in or out.

Oh yes – in the corner there was a bunk as well. On this lay the conker. The sunlight, as it streamed through the iron bars of the window, glinted on its shiny skin. Also it glinted on a tear running down Little Alpesh's cheek. It was visiting time and he'd come to prepare the conker for its trial.

"You can't blame me," said Little Alpesh. "It was all your own fault."

The conker said nothing.

"I mean, you've been asking for trouble right from the start. Why did you have to bash up everything that got in your way? There's no sense to it. And how d'you reckon my Mum and Dad will feel when they arrive home from Pakistan? They've probably told the rest of the family how well they're doing in England – and when they get back they'll find they're the parents of a kid who owns a criminal conker. They'll be so ashamed! What do you say to that?"

Not a word from the conker.

"You'll be shut away for years and years and years, I shouldn't wonder. Already they've taken away your bootlace so you can't batter this place down. Worst of all, I haven't even had a match with you yet. What's the point of owning a conker as hard as a diamond if you don't even have a single conker fight?"

Still there wasn't a peep from the conker. Was it stone-deaf, do you think?

Suddenly there was a rattle at the steel door, followed by the sound of a key as it turned in a lock, the scrape of several bolts being drawn back, the clink of an unravelling chain and the grinding noise of a portcullis – which is a kind of iron grid – as it lifted upwards. The police weren't taking any chances with the conker as hard as a diamond.

"On your feet, son," snapped the sergeant with the ginger beard. "Visiting time is over. His Lordship the Judge wants to see that conker straightaway. Also he wants a word with *you*. Just hold on a tick while I get out my handcuffs."

"Handcuffs?" said Little Alpesh. "But I'm not a prisoner, sir. I'm a witness."

"I know that, son. The handcuffs aren't for you. They're for the conker."

"The conker? How can you handcuff a conker?"

The sergeant smiled grimly.

"Son, I didn't say it would be easy. But this here horror of a horse-chestnut has got to be overpowered before I can take it into court."

"Good luck," said Little Alpesh.

Half an hour later the conker finally hung from the sergeant's left wrist after he'd screwed up the handcuffs as tight as they could get. Even so, the sergeant didn't feel safe and I don't blame him. Would you like to be shackled to a conker so magic it could knock down a multi-storeyed car park and sink a cargo boat? You would? Wait and see what happens, then.

"Hurry up," the sergeant grumbled. "His Lordship the Judge is waiting. Wouldn't be surprised if he doesn't lock up this bleep-bleep, blankety-blank conker and throw away the key. By the time it gets out of gaol it'll be so shrivelled up it'll be smaller than a salted peanut – and serve it right."

His Lordship the Judge wasn't the only one who was waiting. The courtroom was packed out. Almost everyone Little Alpesh knew was there. Next to Big Sister Sameena, for example, sat his rich Uncle Vimesh – who'd shut up his shop especially, though it wasn't even early-closing day. Now Little Alpesh was sure it was serious. As he gazed round at his relatives and friends, at the policeman and court-helpers, at the reporters and at the visitors who were just plain nosey, he realized what it was they were so curious about.

THE CONKER AS HARD AS A DIAMOND.

I expect you know all about courtrooms from films on television, but in case you don't here's what it was like:

There was the Dock (which is where the prisoner sits).

There was the Well-of-the-Court (which is where the helpers sit).

There was the Public Gallery (which is where the watchers sit).

There was the Bench (which is where his Lordship the

Judge sits in his posh robe and crinkly wig).

And there was the Witness Box . . . which is where Little Alpesh sat.

His Lordship the Judge rapped on his desk with a small wooden hammer and the hubbub in the courtroom died down at once.

"Sergeant, be good enough to lift up the prisoner so we can all see it. Now then, first witness, what is your name?"

"Little Alpesh, my Lord."

"And is it true, Little Alpesh, that the Accused – this conker – belongs to you? Was it really given to you by a sort of park-keeper with a wizardy face?"

"Yes," whispered Little Alpesh. "He said I could have it for my very own – provided I promised that whatever happened I didn't get big-headed."

"Big-headed?" the Judge exclaimed. "You must be pin-headed to be the owner of a conker as dangerous as this. Do you admit that so far it has brought about the public clobberation of an old tree, a derelict house, a multi-storeyed car park built back to front, a brand-new council garbage-gobbler and a vast, gleaming, ready-to-sail cargo boat?"

"Yes, my Lord. I'm ever so sorry."

"It's not enough to be sorry, Little Alpesh. You can't nip round to all the things your conker has destroyed and kiss them better, you know. Think yourself lucky nobody was actually hurt. Normally I'd make the prisoner pay for all the damage that's been caused, but since the conker doesn't get any pocket-money I'll have to put it in prison *forever*. Sergeant, hold the prisoner steady, please, while I pass sentence upon it . . . I said keep it still, sergeant. Why are you swinging it backwards and forwards?"

"I'm not, your Lordship," gulped the sergeant. "It seems to be swinging itself."

Which was exactly what was happening, of course. To and fro, to and fro, swung the conker as hard as a diamond. A hush fell over the courtroom as everyone gaped at it.

To and fro, to and fro.

At the end of one of its swings, the conker just managed to *brush* against the prisoner's dock.

CRASH – CLONK – BONKETY – BONK!

Then the conker bounced out of the sergeant's handcuffs, bib-bobbed across the courtroom and just *grazed* the Judge's bench.

CLATTER-BANG!

From here, the conker rolled over the floor until it just *touched* the Public Gallery.

KAPOW!

What an amazing sight . . . in less than the time it takes to dial 999 the whole courtroom was a shambles. Once again, Little Alpesh just couldn't believe it. All round him was smashed-up furniture, a jumble of books and documents, and arms and legs waving in the air. Honestly, he felt so ashamed of his conker he was ready to cry his eyes out. But how could he – in front of all these grown-ups and Uncle Vimesh and Big Sister Sameena? To keep the tears away he blinked.

Blink-blink. Blink-blink. Blink-blink. Blink-blink.

Suddenly . . .

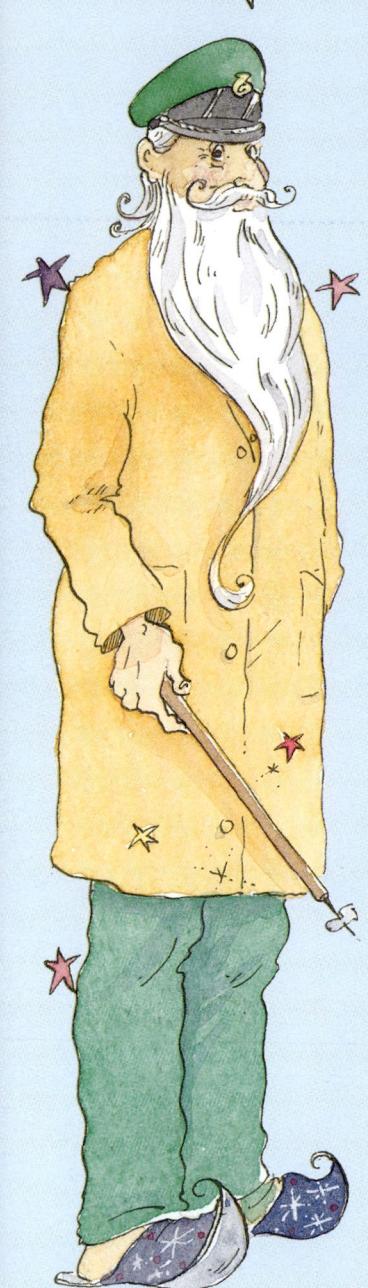

Who was that laughing? Where had Little Alpesh heard that shrill, spooky cackle before? Could it be . . .

"Yes," said a voice. "It's me with the wizardy face again."

There, smack in the middle of the chaos, was an old man who had a park-keeper's uniform, a park-keeper's hat and a stick with a point on the end that was very park-keeperish. Where had he come from? You could see straight away that the Judge wasn't pleased to see him. After all, how happy would you be if your robe was dusty and torn, your wig was skew-whiff, your courtroom totally wrecked and then you were lumbered with a surprise witness?

"What do you want?" his Lordship snarled.

The old man smiled a blustery, gustery, park-keeperish smile.

"First," he said, "I'm here to pay for all the damage caused by the conker as hard as a diamond – every last penny of it. That's only fair since I gave the thing to Little Alpesh in the first place. Second, I'm here to invite you to the Contest."

"The Contest?" snapped the Judge. "What Contest?"

"At this time of the year there's only one Contest worth mentioning," said the old man. "I'm talking about . . . THE CONKER CHAMPIONSHIP OF THE UNIVERSE."

"THE CONKER CHAMPIONSHIP OF THE

UNIVERSE?" gasped Little Alpesh.

"Exactly. It'll be the greatest Contest of its kind that's ever been staged. Already I've had letters from the Queen and the Prime Minister and the Archbishop of Canterbury begging me for tickets. Naturally, I'll do them a favour if I possibly can. But, apart from his Lordship, the most important person there could be *you*, Little Alpesh."

"Me?"

"You and the conker as hard as a diamond."

"We'll... we'll be taking part, you mean?"

"Taking part? Little Alpesh, provided you don't get big-headed, you might even turn out to be the *winner*. What do you say to that?"

Well, if you were Little Alpesh what would you have said? I'll bet your voice would've echoed round the courtroom just as loud and just as long as his did.

"YIPPEEEEEEEEEEEEEE!!!"

Term 2 | Unit 5

Fishing Boats

Fishing boats, called trawlers, have enormous nets, called trawls. This trawler is called a purse seiner. Its net circles the fish and is drawn in by a rope before being winched aboard.

Purse seiner

Stern trawlers haul their nets in from the stern (back of the boat). They are hauled in by mechanical winch.

On board

Once on board, the fish are either packed with ice in boxes or put in huge freezers. Ships with freezers can stay at sea for a long time, without the fish going bad.

Some ships even have fish factories on board. You can find out about them on the next page.

Factory ships

Factory ships have factories on board where the fish are cleaned and prepared for sale. Often smaller fishing boats off-load their haul onto factory ships at sea.

The fish are sent along big square pipes to huge, square trays. Here, a factory worker cleans and prepares the fish.

Some prepared fish are stored in barrels and then stacked on the ship's deck. Others are packed in trays and frozen.

Term 2 | Unit 5

Fish

Fish live in water and are all different shapes and sizes. The enormous whale shark can be up to 15 metres long. A tiny fish called a pygmy goby is no longer than your fingernail. Some fish live in warm, shallow water. Others live in the cold, deep sea.

eye, *fin*, *gill cover*, *fin*, *scale*, *tail*

great white shark

◀ Great white sharks are fast swimmers and fierce hunters. They use their razor-sharp teeth to tear apart their prey.

▼ Blue marlin and many other big fish live far away from the shore. Tuna and mackerel live close to the surface. Sawfish and rays live on the sea bed.

blue marlin

mackerel

tuna

ray

sawfish

108

puffer fish

◀ A puffer fish can blow up its body like a balloon. It does this to scare away its enemies.

▶ The babies of the African cichlid fish swim into their mother's mouth to escape from danger.

African cichlid

1 2 3 4

▲ **1** A female salmon lays her eggs in a river. **2** When the eggs hatch, the babies are called fry.

▲ **3** The young salmon live in the river for two years. **4** Then they swim down to the sea.

▼ Fish that live in the warm, shallow water around coral reefs are often brightly coloured. Their bold patterns help them to hide among the corals and to creep up on their prey.

Fact Box

- A fish is a vertebrate, which means that it has a backbone.
- They breathe by taking in oxygen from the water through their gills.
- Most fish swim through the water by moving their tails from side to side.

Find Out More

- Animals
- Fishing
- Food
- Oceans and seas
- Prehistoric life
- Water

lion fish

butterfly fish

parrot fish

cowfish

angel fish

109

Term 2 | Unit 5

Whales

by Norman Barrett

Toothed whales

The sperm whale, with its unmistakable large, square-shaped head, is by far the largest of the toothed whales. It lives in all the oceans and, like the baleen whales, has been hunted almost to extinction. Sperm whales can stay underwater for over an hour and dive to depths of 1,000m (3,300ft) or more.

There are seven families of toothed whales, and nearly 80 species. Except for the sperm whale, they are mostly small to medium size, and include whales commonly called dolphins and porpoises.

There are toothed whales in all the oceans and seas and also in some rivers. Some species have teeth in both jaws, some in just the upper jaw, and others in just the lower.

Toothed whales can trap and grasp their food. They eat fish and other sea animals. Sperm whales eat octopus and particularly enjoy giant squid 10m (33ft) long.

The pure white beluga whale has a bulging forehead, or "melon". Belugas live in the far north, off Arctic coasts. Their great variety of calls, from clicks and squawks to trills and whistles, earned them the name of sea canary.

The killer whale, or orca, is the largest of the dolphins. It lives mainly on fish and squid, but also preys on seals, seabirds and even other dolphins. Groups of killer whales sometimes combine to attack great baleen whales.

The pilot whale, or blackfish, is a type of dolphin. Pilot whales usually live in large groups, following one or more leaders, or pilots. The picture clearly shows the simple, peg-like teeth common to all toothed whales.

The killer whale is the biggest of the dolphins. It is easily recognized by its large dorsal fin

A Fish of the World *Terry Jones*

A herring once decided to swim right round the world. "I'm tired of the North Sea," he said. "I want to find out what else there is in the world."

So he swam off south into the deep Atlantic. He swam and swam far far away from the seas he knew, through the warm waters of the equator and on down into the South Atlantic. And all the time he saw many strange and wonderful fish that he had never seen before. Once he was nearly eaten by a shark, and once he was nearly electrocuted by an electric eel, and once he was nearly stung by a sting-ray. But he swam on and on, round the tip of Africa and into the Indian Ocean. And he passed by devilfish and sailfish and sawfish and swordfish and bluefish and blackfish and mudfish and sunfish, and he was amazed by the different shapes and sizes and colours.

On he swam, into the Java Sea, and he saw fish that leapt out of the water and fish that lived on the bottom of the sea and fish that could walk on their fins. And on he swam, through the Coral Sea, where the shells of millions and millions of tiny creatures had turned to rock and stood as big as mountains. But still he swam on, into the wide Pacific. He swam over the deepest parts of the ocean, where the water is so deep that it is inky black at the bottom, and the fish carry lanterns over their heads, and some have lights on their tails. And through the Pacific he swam, and then he turned north and headed up to the cold Siberian Sea, where huge white icebergs sailed past him like mighty ships. And still he swam on and on and into the frozen Arctic Ocean, where the sea is for ever covered in ice. And on he went, past Greenland and Iceland, and finally he swam home into his own North Sea.

All his friends and relations gathered round and made a great fuss of him. They had a big feast and offered him the very best food they could find. But the herring just yawned and said: "I've swum round the entire world. I have seen everything there is to see, and I have eaten more exotic and wonderful dishes than you could possibly imagine." And he refused to eat anything.

Then his friends and relations begged him to come home and live with them, but he refused. "I've been everywhere there is, and that old rock is too dull and small for me." And he went off and lived on his own.

And when the breeding season came, he refused to join in the spawning, saying: "I've swum around the entire world, and now I know how many fish there are in the world, I can't be interested in herrings anymore."

Eventually, one of the oldest of the herrings swam up to him, and said: "Listen. If you don't spawn with us, some herrings' eggs will go unfertilized and will not turn into healthy young herrings. If you don't live with your family, you'll make them sad. And if you don't eat, you'll die."

But the herring said: "I don't mind. I've been everywhere there is to go, I've seen everything there is to see, and now I know everything there is to know."

The old fish shook his head. "No one has ever seen everything there is to see," he said, "nor known everything there is to know."

"Look," said the herring, "I've swum through the North Sea, the Atlantic Ocean, the Indian Ocean, the Java Sea, the Coral Sea, the great Pacific Ocean, the Siberian Sea and the frozen Arctic. Tell me, what else is there for me to see or know?"

"I don't know," said the old herring, "but there may be something."

Well, just then, a fishing-boat came by, and all the herrings were caught in a net and taken to market that very day. And a man bought the herring, and ate it for his supper.

And he never knew that it had swum right round the world, and had seen everything there was to see, and knew everything there was to know.

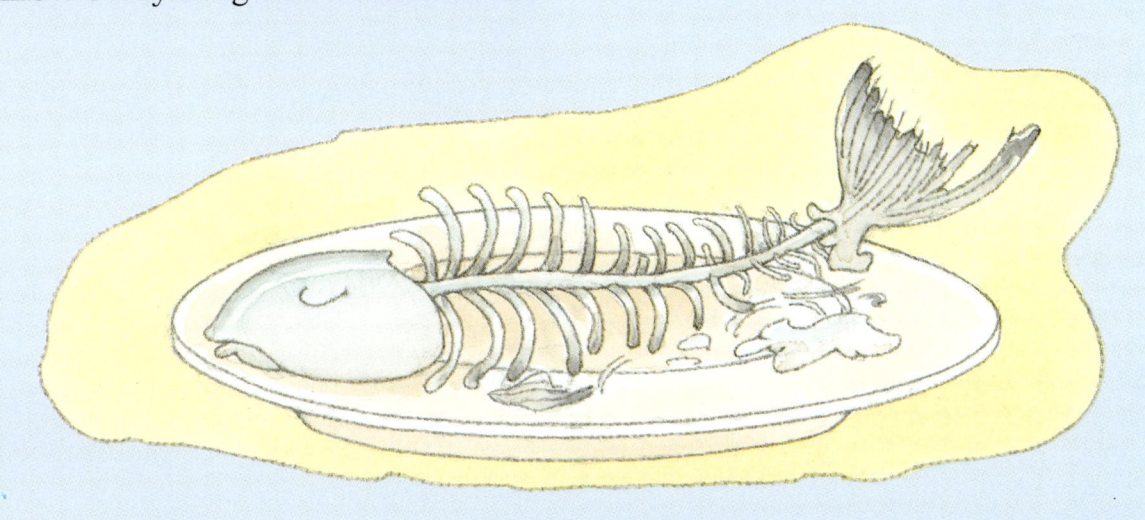

Colin

When you frown at me like that, Colin,
and wave your arm in the air,
I know just what you're going to say:
"Please, Sir, it isn't fair!"

It isn't fair
On the football field
If their team scores a goal.
It isn't fair
In a cricket match
Unless you bat *and* bowl.

When you scowl at me that way, Colin,
And mutter and slam your chair,
I always know what's coming next:
"Please, Sir, it isn't fair!"

It isn't fair
When I give you a job.
It isn't fair when I don't.
If I keep you in
It isn't fair.
If you're told to go out, you won't.

When heads bow low in assembly
And the whole school's saying a prayer,
I can guess what's on your mind, Colin:
"Our Father . . . it isn't fair!"

It wasn't fair
In the Infants.
It isn't fair now.
It won't be fair
At the Comprehensive
(For first years, anyhow).

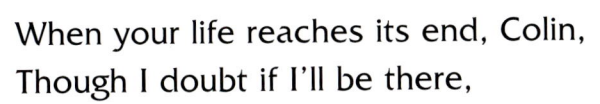

When your life reaches its end, Colin,
Though I doubt if I'll be there,
I can picture the words on the gravestone now.
They'll say: IT IS NOT FAIR.

Allan Ahlberg

Please Mrs Butler

Please Mrs Butler
This boy Derek Drew
Keeps copying my work, Miss.
What shall I do?

Go and sit in the hall, dear.
Go and sit in the sink.
Take your books on the roof, my lamb.
Do whatever you think.

Please Mrs Butler
This boy Derek Drew
Keeps taking my rubber, Miss.
What shall I do?

Keep it in your hand, dear.
Hide it up your vest.
Swallow it if you like, my love.
Do what you think best.

Please Mrs Butler
This boy Derek Drew
Keeps calling me rude names, Miss.
What shall I do?

Lock yourself in the cupboard, dear.
Run away to sea.
Do whatever you can, my flower.
But *don't ask me!*

Allan Ahlberg

A Schoolmaster's Admonition

Good children, refuse not these lessons to learn,
The pathway to virtue you here may discern;
In keeping them truly you shall be most sure
The praise of all people thereby to procure.

Be comely and decent in all thy array,
Not wantonly given to sport and to play;
But labour by virtue, in youth, to obtain
The love of thy betters, their friendship to gain.

The morning appearing, rise thou with speed,
Wash hands and face cleanly before thou go feed;
Let shoes be fast tied both, close to thy feet,
The better to travel all day in the street.

If thou be a scholar, to school make good haste,
For he is a truant that cometh there last;
For if thou dost loiter and play by the way,
Be sure with thy master it will cause a fray.

Swear not, nor curse not; delight not to steal;
Thy master obey thou; his secrets conceal;
Take heed of false lying; set no man at strife;
Nor be thou too desperate to strike with a knife.

And now, to conclude, bear this well in mind,
A diligent scholar much favour shall find;
But such as will loiter, and lazy will be,
Shall for their labour be brought on their knee.

Anon (1625)

Demeanour

Busy in study be thou, child,
And in the hall, meek and mild,
And at the table, merry and glad,
And at bed, soft and sad.

Anon (c. 1525)

The Dunce

Why does he still keep ticking?
   Why does his round white face
Stare at me over the books and ink,
   And mock at my disgrace?
Why does that thrush call, "Dunce, dunce, dunce!"?
   Why does that bluebottle buzz?
Why does the sun so silent shine? –
   And what do I care if it does?

Walter de la Mare

The Outing

Right, class six
RIGHT, CLASS SIX
I'm talking

I'm talking
I want complete quiet
and that includes you,
   David Alexander,
yes, you
no need to turn around, David
there aren't any other
   David Alexanders here,
   are there?

Louise
it isn't absolutely necessary
        for your watch
to play us London's Burning
        just now, is it?

Right
as you know
it was our plan to go out today –
to the Science Museum.
Now I had hoped that it would
        not be necessary
for me to have to tell you –
yes, you as well, Abdul,
you're in class six as well, aren't you?
I saw that, Mark,
I saw it.
Any more and you'll be out.
No trip,
nothing.

I had hoped that it
        wouldn't be necessary
for me to tell you how
        to BEHAVE
when we go on a trip.

But –
and this is a big but –
you haven't heard a word I've
        said, have you, Donna?

This is a big but
I HAVE to tell you how to
    behave, don't I?
Why?

Yes, it IS because you never listen
but there's another reason, isn't there?
Yes, Warren,
because of what happened last time.

Let us remind ourselves of a few things:
The food –
Even as I speak
would you believe it?
I can see that Phanh has opened her
    can of drink
I do not believe it
I really don't.
Do we have lunch at nine-thirty
    at school?
No,
we have lunch at twelve fifteen
but, Phanh, you've already
    begun yours.

If you remember,
last time
Joanna had eaten all her sandwiches
before she even got to school.

Lloyd sat on his orange
and burst it
and Alfred put a chocolate swiss
    roll in his pocket
and –
yes –
it melted.

So, remember, lunch is when?
yes yes yes
of course lunch is at lunch time
but when?
twelve fifteen
correct

Perhaps, I thought,
when I got up this morning,
I won't have to tell class six
about what to do when we get
    to the station
but I remembered
David's little gang
who decided they wouldn't wait
    for me to tell them
what train to get on
and before we all knew it
David and his little gang
were heading for the seaside
    on their own.

When we get to the museum –
Of course YOU'RE not
 listening, are you, Lydia?
But then of course you didn't
 listen last time, did you?
And then you wondered why
you sat on Lloyd's orange after
 Lloyd had already sat on it once.

When we get to the museum
do we run about the corridors?
Do we run around screaming?
Do we go sliding on the shiny floors?
No we don't
no we don't
no we don't.

Thank you, Mervyn, that's enough
I'm very glad you've got jam
 in your sandwiches, Mervyn,
we are all glad that you've got jam
 in your sandwiches, Mervyn,
but what has it got to do with
 sliding on the floor of the
 Science Museum?
Precisely nothing.
I'm very sorry, Mervyn, but nobody,
nobody at all
wants to know about the jam
 in your sandwiches, Mervyn.

Now,
when you're ready
when you're quiet
we'll all go.
That doesn't mean leaping up
    in the air, Karen, does it?
Louise, why is your watch now
    playing
For He's A Jolly Good Fellow?
Yes, I know it could be SHE'S A
Jolly Good Fellow, Zoe,
but that isn't what we are talking
    about, is it?

Mervyn,
if I hear about your sandwiches
your jam
or the jam IN your sandwiches
if I hear about any of it once more
I shall give them to the ducks.

Yes, John, what do you want?
I don't know what ducks, John.
Any ducks.

Right
when there is complete quiet
complete quiet
you will find your partners and stand by the door.

Oh no, not another
chocolate swiss roll,
Alfred, surely not?

Marcia, you cannot have
Charmaine AND
Donna
as your partner
because that makes three
and three does not mean
PARTNER, does it?
And perhaps you can put
your comb in your bag for
at least three seconds
just giving us enough time
to get to the door? Mmm?

Good
right, class six, we're off

Why not leave your watch
behind, Louise?

Michael Rosen

Term 2 | Unit 8

The Knowhow Book of Print and Paint

by Heather Avery and Anne Cwardi

Before You Start

These are the things you need to make the prints in this book:

Paint – powder or poster paints are good for printing.

Paper – use drawing paper for the best prints. Practise printing on rough paper. Try using rolls of white shelf paper, wall lining paper or the back of a roll of old wallpaper. Some art shops sell sheets of thick, cheap paper called sugar paper.

Coloured card – for picture frames. Stationery and art shops sell sheets of brightly coloured card.

Waterproof inks – these are made by Reeves and Windsor & Newton. They are sold in stationery and art shops.

Fabric dyes – ask in art or craft shops for water-based dyes, such as Reeves Craft Dye. You have to buy a fixer for this dye. Read the instructions on the bottles carefully.

Glitter – you can buy tubes of different colours at toy or stationery shops.

Expanded polystyrene – this white, light plastic stuff is often used for packing breakable things. Try asking for some in a shop or store. Use thick pieces for printing blocks.

Sheet sponge – this artificial sponge is usually sold in Woolworth's and furniture stores. Use it to dab on paint and to make sponge rollers.

Paste – for paint and paste prints, use any good paste.

Glue – use any good glue to stick cardboard and sponge rollers.

Black Indian ink – this is sold by stationery and art shops.

Water-based block printing colours – these are made by Reeves and are good for monoprints.

128

Getting Ready

Printing and painting can be a messy business, so it is a good idea to get everything ready before you start. Cover a table or bench with lots of newspaper and put it over any furniture which could be splashed with paint. If you are making very long prints on rolls of paper, put newspaper on the floor and use it as a working surface. Wear old clothes or something over your clothes. An old shirt makes a good painting smock. Collect all the things you will need for one kind of printing and have them ready to use. Rags are useful for wiping paint off your hands and mopping up spilled paint or ink. When you have made a print, hang it up or lay it down flat to dry. Remember to clear up when you have finished printing. Put the tops on bottles and tubes of paint and wash the brushes.

Term 2 | Unit 8

About this book

Cartoons look quick and easy to draw. You may have found that they are not as easy as they look, though. This book is full of simple ways to do good cartoons.

The first part tells you how to draw cartoon people using simple shapes and lines. You can find out how to draw expressions and movement, too.

A caricature is a funny picture of a real person. You exaggerate things, such as the shape of their nose or hair. You can find out how to do this on pages 8–9.

A strip cartoon is a series of pictures which tell a joke or funny short story. You can find out how to build up your own strip cartoons on pages 24–25.

130

Looking at a cartoon story book is a bit like watching a film and reading a book at the same time. You can see how the Tintin stories were created on pages 30–31.

On pages 34–37, you can find out how cartoon films are made. This is called animation, which means "the giving of life". Cartoons are brought to life in a film.

The Not-Very-Nice-Prince

by Pamela Oldfield

Prince Ferdinand was not very nice and hardly anybody liked him. Only the Princess Eglantine could put up with his rude manners, and they would visit each other from time to time for a game of Snakes and Ladders.

One day the Prince was driving home in the royal coach when it came to a sudden halt. An old woman was crossing the road with an ancient pram laden with firewood.

The Prince put his head out of the window and shouted at her. "I say, old woman, move that flipping pram out of my way and look sharp about it."

The old woman looked at him. She was very ugly indeed and in need of a good wash.

"Hang on a minute, your Highness," she croaked. "This nearside wheel's a bit wobbly . . ."

Now a gentleman would have offered to help her but Prince Ferdinand was no gentleman.

"Don't bother me with your excuses," he shouted. "Get the flipping thing out of my way."

Well, the ugly old woman was really a witch. She didn't

like his manners and decided to teach him a lesson. She pointed at him with a long bony finger and muttered some magic words. He heard the word "flipping" but that was all.

At once the "flipping thing" flipped. To Ferdinand's dismay the pram rose into the air and turned right over. All the firewood fell out on to the startled horses.

They were very frightened and promptly ran away and the coach came unhitched and rolled into the hedge. The Prince climbed out of his wrecked coach and looked for the old woman but she had disappeared. He didn't know that she had put a spell on him.

But the next day a girl came to the door with a basket of eggs.

"Good day to your Highness," she said politely. "Will you buy some new-laid eggs?"

"No, I won't," he said without even a thank you.

"But they are beautiful brown eggs," she said.

"They may be sky-blue pink for all I care," he said. "Take the flipping things away."

You can guess what happened!

The basket rose up into the air and turned over. The eggs fell on the Prince's best velvet coat and ruined it.

"Now I see it all!" he cried fearfully. "The old woman was a witch and she has put a spell on me. I shall have to be very careful what I say from now on."

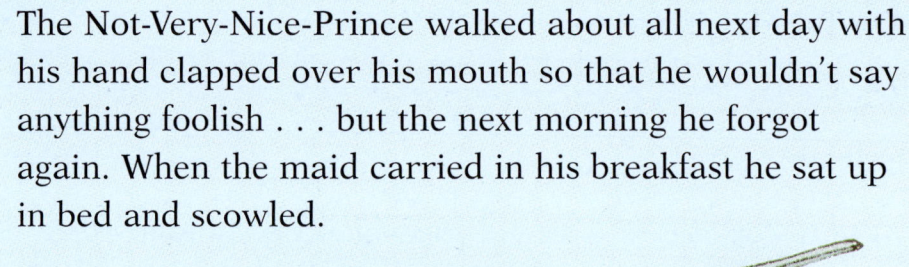

The Not-Very-Nice-Prince walked about all next day with his hand clapped over his mouth so that he wouldn't say anything foolish . . . but the next morning he forgot again. When the maid carried in his breakfast he sat up in bed and scowled.

"What on earth is that?" he asked.

"Crunchy Pops, your Highness."

"Crunchy Pops!" he grumbled. "I wanted eggs and bacon. Take the flipping things – Ooh!"

Too late he realised what he'd said. The bowl of Crunchy Pops floated into the air and flipped right over. It emptied itself all over his head. Prince Ferdinand screamed with rage and the terrified maid fled into a nearby broom cupboard and wept copiously.

After that, things went from bad to worse. The Prince became very flustered and that made him even more forgetful. On Monday he flipped a royal banquet.

On Tuesday it was a market stall.

On Wednesday it was a troop of the King's best soldiers!

But he had finally gone too far.

"Get out of my sight," roared the King, stamping his foot so hard that it hurt.

"Don't come back until the spell is lifted."

Notices were put up warning people to keep away from the Prince and they didn't need telling twice.

So the unfortunate Ferdinand retired to a dark dungeon below the palace and wondered what he should do. He didn't tell anyone where he was and no one bothered to find out – which was very sad.

One day the Princess Eglantine visited the King for a game of croquet. She had almost won the game when she caught sight of the Prince watching them from the dungeon. Kindly, she offered to visit him for a game of Snakes and Ladders.

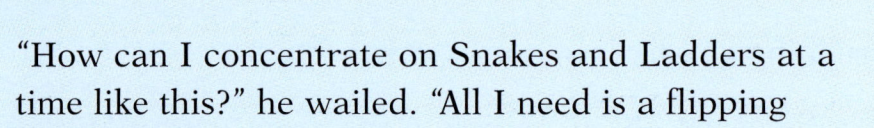

"How can I concentrate on Snakes and Ladders at a time like this?" he wailed. "All I need is a flipping Princess who –"

He had done it again! Slowly the Princess rose in the air and turned over.

She came down on her bottom and everyone laughed.

The Princess was mortified. "I shall be back when the spell is lifted and *not* before," she told the King, and stomped off home with her nose in the air.

The question was – who could lift the spell? The only visitor to the dark dungeon was an old woman who took him bread and water each day. Prince Ferdinand was so busy feeling sorry for himself he didn't even recognize her. He had plenty of time to ponder his manners and vowed that if the spell were ever lifted he would be a reformed character.

One day the old woman, who was really the witch, came into the dungeon. She had a pail of water and a scrubbing brush and she began to scrub the floor. The Prince looked at her kindly.

"That is hard work for an old woman," he said politely. "Please let me help you."

To the old woman's dismay he seized the scrubbing brush and fell to scrubbing the dungeon floor. She stared at him in horror.

"You nincompoop!" she roared. "You numbskull! Why do you have to be so polite? Your cursed good manners have lifted the spell – and broken my power also . . . Aah!"

And she vanished in a puff of horrid green smoke which smelled like burnt kippers.

Of course, the people were delighted. They carried Ferdinand through the streets rejoicing – all the way to the Princess Eglantine's palace. She was waiting eagerly for the Very-Nice-Prince and another game of Snakes and Ladders.

Term 2 | Unit 10

Savitri and Satyavan

by Madhur Jaffrey

Once upon a time there lived a King and Queen, who after many years of being childless, gave birth to a daughter.

She was the most beautiful baby the parents could have hoped for, and they named her Savitri.

When Savitri grew up and it was time for her to marry, her father said to her, "Dearest child, we have to part with you. You have given us the greatest joy that humans can ever know. But it is time for you to start a family of your own. Is there any man you wish to marry?"

"No, father," replied Savitri, "I have not yet met a man I would care to spend my life with."

"Perhaps we should send for pictures of all the nobles in the country. You might come upon a face you like." said the King and he sent his court painter to bring back portraits of all the nobles and rulers in the country.

Savitri examined the portraits, one after the other, and shook her head. The men in the portraits all looked so very ordinary, even though they were all emperors, kings and princes.

The King then said to his daughter, "It might be best if

you went to all the big cities of the world to find a husband for yourself. I will provide you with the proper escort of men, elephants, camels and horses. Good luck. I hope you can find a man to love."

Savitri set out with a large procession of men, elephants, camels and horses. In her effort to visit all the cities of the world, she had to cross many oceans and deserts. She did this fearlessly. But she never found a man she could love.

When she returned home, her father said to her, "You have looked in all the big cities of the world and have found no man that you wish to marry, perhaps you should now search through all the forests of the world."

Savitri set out again with a large procession of men, elephants, camels and horses, and began searching through all the forests of the world. She did this fearlessly.

She had looked through the last forest and was just about to return home when she came upon a young man who was cutting wood.

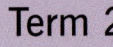

"What is your name?" she asked.

"Satyavan, your highness," he replied

"Please do not address me as 'your highness'," she said, "my name is Savitri. What do you do for a living?"

"I do nothing much," the young man replied. "I have very old, blind parents. I live with them in a small, thatched cottage at the edge of the forest. Every morning I go out to cut wood and gather food. In the evening I make a fire for my parents, cook their dinner, and feed them. That is all I do."

Savitri returned to her father's palace and said, "Dearest mother and father. I have finally found a man to love and marry. His name is Satyavan and he lives in a cottage by a forest not too far from here."

"But will you be able to live a simple life in a simple cottage?" asked her father. "This man obviously has no money."

"That makes no difference at all to me," Savitri said. "He is capable, honest, good and caring. That is what I respect and love him for."

The King sent a messenger to the blind couple's cottage saying that Princess Savitri wished to marry their son, Satyavan. When Satyavan arrived home that evening with his heavy load of wood his parents said, "There are messengers here from the King. Princess Savitri wishes to marry you."

"I love the young lady in question," replied Satyavan, "but I cannot marry her. She has money, jewels, elephants, camels and servants. What can I offer her?"

Tears rolled down the faces of his blind parents. "Son," cried his mother, "we never told you this, but long ago, before you were born, your father too was a ruler with a kingdom of his own. His wicked brother blinded us and stole our birthright. You should have been born a prince and heir to the kingdom, quite worthy of Savitri. We have fallen on hard times, but if you two love each other, why should you not marry? Who knows what the future has in store for anybody?"

Term 2 | Unit 10

So a message was sent back to the King saying that Satyavan had agreed to the match.

On the day of the wedding, the King and Queen held a huge reception. Everyone of importance was invited.

That is how it happened that the wisest sage in the kingdom appeared at the scene.

Just before the wedding ceremony, the sage took the King and Queen aside and whispered, "It is my duty to warn you. The young man your daughter is to marry is decent and of good character, but his stars are crossed. He will die very shortly. This marriage would be a tragic mistake."

The King felt ill when he heard this. He called his daughter and told her what the sage had said, adding,

"Perhaps it is best to call the marriage off."

"No, father," Savitri said solemnly, "I will marry Satyavan, whatever our future may hold."

Savitri was no fool, however. She had heard that the sage knew of heavenly remedies for earthly problems.

"Oh dearest sage," Savitri said to him, "surely there is a way I can prevent my husband from dying. You, in your great wisdom, must offer me some hope. There must be something I can do?"

The sage thought deeply, "You can extend your husband's life by fasting. Eat nothing but fruit, roots and leaves for a year, and Satyavan will live for those twelve months. After that he must die."

With a sense of doom hanging over the bride's family, the wedding did take place. The groom and his parents were told nothing of what the future held for them.

Savitri began to lead a simple life with her husband and parents-in-law. Early each morning, Satyavan set out for the forest to cut wood and to forage for food. When he was gone, Savitri made the beds, swept the house, and shepherded her in-laws around wherever they wished to go. She also prayed and fasted.

One day Savitri's mother-in-law said to her, "Child, we know how rich a family you come from. Since we have lost our kingdom, we can offer you no fineries but Satyavan does collect enough food for all of us. We have noticed that you eat just fruit, roots and leaves and never touch any grain. That is not a healthy diet. We are beginning to worry about you."

"Oh, please don't worry about me," begged Savitri. "I love to eat fruit."

The twelve months were almost over. On the very last day, Savitri got up with her husband and announced that she would accompany him into the forest.

"Child, what will you do in the forest? The work is hard and there are all kinds of dangerous animals," said her mother-in-law.

"Do stay at home," said Satyavan, "The forest is not a comfortable place."

"I have travelled through all the forests of the world. I was not uncomfortable and I was not frightened. Let me go with you today."

Satyavan had no answer for his wife. He loved her a lot and trusted her instincts. "Come along then, we'd better start quickly. The sun is almost up."

So they set out towards the heart of the forest.

Once there, Satyavan climbed a tree and began to saw off its dried-up branches.

It was a scorching hot day in May. The trees had shed the last withered yellowing leaves. Savitri looked for a cool spot to sit down and just could not find any. Her heart was beating like a two-sided drum. Any moment now the year would end.

"Ahhh . . ." came a cry from Satyavan.

Savitri ran towards him, "Are you all right?"

"I have a piercing headache."

"Come down from the tree. It's the

heat. I will run and find some shade." Savitri found a banyan tree and helped Satyavan towards it. Many of the banyan tree's branches had gone deep into the earth and come up again to form a deliciously cool grove. The leaves rustled gently to fan the couple.

"Put your head in my lap," Savitri said to Satyavan, "and rest."

Satyavan put his head down, gave a low moan, and died.

Savitri looked up. There, in the distance coming towards her was Yamraj, the King of the Underworld. He was riding a male water buffalo, and Savitri knew he was coming to claim Satyavan's soul. She turned to the banyan tree and implored, "Banyan tree, banyan tree, look after my husband. Shield him and keep him cool. I will return one day to claim him."

Yamraj took Satyavan's soul and started to ride away. Savitri followed on foot. She followed for miles and miles. Yamraj finally turned around and said, "Why are you following me, woman?"

"You are taking my husband's soul away. Why don't you take me as well? I cannot live without him."

"Go back, go back to your home and do not bother me," Yamraj said.

But Savitri kept following.

Yamraj turned around again. "Stop following me, woman," he cried.

Savitri paid no heed to him.

"Well, woman," said Yamraj, "I can see that you are quite determined. I will grant you just one wish. As long as you do not ask for your husband's soul."

"May my in-laws have their sight back?" asked Savitri.

"All right, all right," said Yamraj, "now go home."

After several more miles Yamraj glanced back. There was Savitri, still following.

"You really are quite persistent," Yamraj said. "I'll grant you one other wish. Just remember do not ask for your husband's soul."

"Could my father-in-law get back the kingdom he lost?" Savitri asked.

"Yes, yes," said Yamraj, "now go, go."

Several miles later, Yamraj looked back again.

Savitri was still following.

"I do not understand you. I've granted you two wishes and yet you keep following me. This is the last wish I am offering you. Remember you can ask for anything but your husband's soul."

"May I be the mother of many sons?" Savitri asked.

"Yes, yes," Yamraj said. "Now go. Go back home."

Several miles later Yamraj looked back only to see Savitri still there. "Why are you still following me?" Yamraj asked. "I have already granted your wish of many sons."

"How will I have many sons?" Savritri asked. "You have the soul of the only husband I have. I will never marry again. You have granted me a false wish. It can never come true."

"I have had enough," Yamraj said. "I am quite exhausted. Here, take back your husband's soul."

Savitri rushed back to the banyan tree so her husband's body and soul could be joined again.

"Oh banyan tree," she said, "thank you for looking after my husband. In the years to come, may all married women come to you and offer thanks and prayers."

Satyavan opened his eyes and said, "My headache has gone."

"Yes," said Savitri, "thanks to the kind banyan tree that offered us its shade. Let us go home now where a surprise awaits you. I will not tell you what it is."

Satyavan put his arm around his wife's shoulders and they began to walk slowly back home.

Once There Were No Pandas

by Margaret Greaves

Long, long ago in China, when the earth and the stars were young, there were none of the black-and-white bears, that the Chinese call *Xiong mao* and that we call "pandas". But deep in the bamboo forests lived bears with fur as white and soft and shining as new-fallen snow. The Chinese called them *Bai xiong* which means "white bear".

In a small house at the edge of the forest lived a peasant and his wife and their little daughter, Chien-min.

One very hot day, Chien-min was playing alone at the edge of the forest. The green shadow of the trees looked cool as water, and a patch of yellow buttercups shone invitingly.

"They are only *just* inside the forest," said the little girl to herself. "It will take only a minute to pick some."

She slipped in among the trees. But when she had picked the flowers, she looked around puzzled. There were so many small paths! Which one led back to the village?

As she hesitated, something moved and rustled among the leaves nearby. She saw a delicate head with big ears, a slim body dappled with light and shadow. It was one of the small deer of the forest. Chien-min had startled it, and it bounded away between the trees. She tried to follow, hoping it might lead her home. But almost at once it was out of sight, and Chien-min was completely lost.

She began to be frightened. But then she heard another sound – something whimpering not far away. She ran towards the place, forgetting her fear, wanting only to help.

There, close to a big thorny bush, squatted a very small white bear cub. Every now and then he shook one of his front paws and licked it, then whimpered again.

"Oh, you poor little one!" Chien-min ran over and knelt beside the little bear. "Don't cry! I'll help you. Let me see it."

The little cub seemed to understand. He let her take hold of his paw. Between the pads was a very sharp thorn. Chien-min pinched it between her finger and thumb, and very carefully drew it out. The cub rubbed his head against her hands as she stroked him.

A moment later, a huge white bear came crashing through the trees, growling fiercely. But when she saw that the little girl was only playing with her cub, her anger vanished. She licked his paw, then nuzzled Chien-min as if she too were one of her cubs.

The mother bear was so gentle that the child took courage and put her arms round her neck, stroking the soft fur. "How beautiful you are!" Chien-min said, "Oh, if only you could show me the way home."

At once the great bear ambled forward, grunting to the cub and his new friend to follow. Fearlessly now, Chien-min held on to her thick white coat and very soon found that she was at the edge of the forest again, close to her own home.

From that day on, she often went into the forest. Her parents were happy about it, knowing their daughter was safe under the protection of the great white bear. She met many of the other bears too, and many of their young, but her special friend was always the little cub she had helped. She called him *Niao Niao*, which means "very soft", because his fur was so fine and beautiful.

The mother bear even showed the little girl her secret home, a den in the hollow of a great tree. Chien-min went there many times, played with the cubs, and learned the ways of the forest. Always the great she-bear led her safely back before nightfall.

One warm spring afternoon, Chien-min was sitting by the hollow tree, watching the cubs play, when she saw a stealthy movement between the bamboos. A wide, whiskered face. Fierce topaz eyes. Small tufted ears. A glimpse of spotted, silky fur.

Chien-min sprang up, shouting a warning. But she was too late. With bared teeth and lashing tail, the hungry leopard had leaped upon Niao Niao.

Chien-min forgot all her fear in her love for her friend. Snatching up a great stone, she hurled it at the leopard. The savage beast dropped his prey but turned on her, snarling with fury. At the same moment, the she-bear charged through the trees like a thunderbolt.

The leopard backed off, terrified by her anger. But as he turned to run, he struck out at Chien-min with his huge claws, knocking her to the ground.

The bears ran to Chien-min, growling and whining and licking her face, but the little girl never moved. She had saved Niao Niao's life by the loss of her own.

News of her death swept through the forest. From miles away, north, south, east and west, all the white bears gathered to mourn. They wept and whimpered for their lost friend, rubbing their paws in the dust of the earth and wiping the tears from their eyes. As they did so, the wet dust left great black smears across their faces. They beat their paws against their bodies in bitter lamentation, and the wet dust clung to their fur in wide black bands.

But although the bears sorrowed for Chien-min, and her parents and friends mourned her, they were all comforted to know that she was happy. Guan-yin, the beautiful Goddess of Mercy, would give her a special place in heaven, where her selfless love for her friend would always be rewarded.

And from that day to this, there have been no white bears, *Bai xiong,* anywhere in China. Instead there are the great black-and-white bears, *Xiong mao,* that we call "pandas", still in mourning for their lost friend, Chien-min.

Term 2 | Unit 12

Brazilian Footballer

Pelé kicked in his mother's belly!
And the world shouted:
Gooooooooooooooooooooooooooooal!
When her son was born,
He became the sun,
And rolled on the fields of heaven.
The moon and stars trained and coached him,
In the milky way
He swayed, danced and dribbled,
Smooth like water off a duck's back
Ready always to attack.
One hot day, heaven fell down, floored!
Through the Almighty's hands
Pelé had scored!

Faustin Charles

Hurricane

Shut the windows
Bolt the doors
Big rain coming
Climbing up the mountain

Neighbours whisper
Dark clouds gather
Big rain coming
Climbing up the mountain

Gather in the clotheslines
Pull down the blinds
Big wind rising
Coming up the mountain

Branches falling
Raindrops flying
Treetops swaying
People running
Big wind blowing
Hurricane! on the mountain.

Dionne Brand

Isn't My Name Magical?

Nobody can see my name on me.
My name is inside
and all over me, unseen
like other people also keep it.
Isn't my name magical?

My name is mine only.
It tells I am individual,
the one special person it shakes
when I'm wanted.

Even if someone else answers
for me, my message hangs in air
haunting others, till it stops
with me, the right name.
Isn't your name and my name magic?

If I'm with hundreds of people
and my name gets called,
my sound switches me on to answer
like it was my human electricity.

My name echoes across playground,
it comes, it demands my attention.
I have to find out who calls,
who wants me for what.
My name gets blurted out in class,
it is terror, at a bad time,
because somebody is cross.

My name gets called in a whisper
I am happy, because
my name may have touched me
with a loving voice.
Isn't your name and my name magic?

James Berry

Chicken Dinner

Mama, don' do it, please,
Don' cook dat chicken fe dinner,
We know dat chicken from she hatch,
She is de only one in de batch
Dat de mongoose didn' catch,
Please don' cook her fe dinner.

Mama, don' do it, please,
Don' cook dat chicken fe dinner,
Yuh mean to tell mi yuh feget
Yuh promise her to we as a pet
She not even have a chance to lay yet
An yuh want to cook her fe dinner.

Mama, don' do it, please,
Don' cook dat chicken fe dinner,
Don' give Henrietta de chop,
Ah tell yuh what, we could swop,
We will get yuh one from de shop,
If yuh promise not to cook her fe dinner.

Mama, me really glad, yuh know,
Yuh never cook Henny fe dinner,
An she glad too, ah bet,
Oh Lawd, me suddenly feel upset,
Yuh don' suppose is somebody else pet
We eating now fe dinner?

Valerie Bloom

Cheating

by Susan Shreve

I cheated on a unit test in maths this morning during the second period with Mr Burke. Afterwards, I was too sick to eat lunch just thinking about it.

I came straight home from school, went to my room, and lay on the floor trying to decide whether it would be better to run away from home now or after supper. Mostly I wished I was dead.

It wasn't even an accident that I cheated.

Yesterday Mr Burke announced there'd be a unit test and anyone who didn't pass would have to come to school on Saturday, most particularly me, since I didn't pass the last unit test. He said that right out in front of everyone as usual. You can imagine how much I like Mr Burke.

But I did plan to study just to prove to him that I'm pretty clever – which I am mostly – except in maths, which I'd be okay in if I'd memorize my times tables. Anyway, I got my desk ready to study on since it was stacked with about two million things. Just when I was ready to work, Nicho came into my room with our new rabbit and it jumped on my desk and knocked the flash cards all over the floor.

I yelled for my mother to come and help me pick them up, but Carlotta was crying as usual and Mother said I was old enough to help myself and a bunch of other stuff like that which mothers like to say. My mother's one of those people who tells you everything you've done wrong for thirty years like you do it every day. It drives me crazy.

Anyway, Nicho and I took the rabbit outside, but then Philip came to my room and also Marty from next door, and before long it was dinner. After dinner my father said I could watch a special on television if I'd done all my homework.

Of course I said I had.

That was the beginning. I felt terrible telling my father a lie about the homework so I couldn't even enjoy the special. I think he knew I was lying and was so disappointed he couldn't talk about it.

Not much is important in our family. Marty's mother wants him to look okay all the time and my friend Nathan has to do well at school and Andy has so many rules he must go crazy just trying to remember them. My parents don't bother making up a lot of rules. But we do have to tell the truth – even if it's bad, which it usually is. You can imagine how I didn't really enjoy the special.

It was nine o'clock when I got up to my room and that was too late to study for the unit test so I lay in my bed with the light off and decided what I would do the next day when I was in Mr B's maths class not knowing the eight- and nine-times tables.

So, you see, the cheating was planned after all.

But at night, thinking about Mr B – who could scare just about anybody I know, even my father – it seemed perfectly sensible to cheat. It didn't even seem bad when I thought of my parents' big thing about telling the truth.

I'd go into class jolly as usual, acting like things were going just great, and no one, not even Mr B, would suspect the truth. I'd sit down next to Stanley Plummer – he is so clever at maths it makes you sick – and from time to time, I'd glance over at his paper to copy the answers. It would be a cinch. In fact, every test before, I had to try hard not to see his answers because our desks are practically on top of each other.

And that's exactly what I did this morning. It was a cinch. Everything was okay except that my stomach was upside down and I wanted to die.

The fact is, I couldn't believe what I'd done in cold blood. I began to wonder about myself – really wonder – things like whether I would steal from shops or hurt someone on purpose or do some other terrible thing I couldn't even imagine. I began to wonder whether I was just bad to the core.

I've never been a wonderful kid that everybody in the world loves and thinks is great, like Nicho. I have a bad temper and I like to have my own way and I argue a lot. Sometimes I can be mean. But most of the time I've thought of myself as a pretty decent kid. Mostly I work hard, I stick up for little kids, and I tell the truth. Mostly I like myself fine – except I wish I were better at basketball.

Now all of a sudden I've turned into this criminal. It's hard to believe I'm just a boy. And all because of one stupid maths test.

Lying on the floor of my room, I begin to think that probably I've been bad all along. It just took this maths test to clinch it. I'll probably never tell the truth again.

I tell my mother I'm ill when she calls me to come down for dinner. She doesn't believe me, but puts me to bed anyhow. I lie there in the early winter darkness, wondering what terrible thing I'll be doing next, when my father comes in and sits down on my bed.

"What's the matter?" he asks.

"I've got a stomach ache," I say. Luckily, it's too dark to see his face.

"Is that all?"

"Yeah."

"Mummy says you've been in your room since school."

"I was sick there, too," I say.

"She thinks something happened today and you're upset."

That's the thing that really drives me crazy about my mother. She knows things sitting inside my head the same as if I was turned inside out.

"Well," my father says. I can tell he doesn't believe me.

"My stomach *is* feeling sort of upset," I hedge.

"Okay," he says and he pats my leg and gets up.

Just as he shuts the door to my room I call out to him in a voice I don't even recognize as my own that I'm going to have to run away.

"How come?" he calls back, not surprised or anything.

So I tell him I cheated in the maths test. To tell the truth, I'm surprised at myself. I didn't plan to tell him anything.

He doesn't say anything at first and that just about kills me. I'd be fine if he'd spank me or something. To say nothing can drive a person crazy.

And then he says I'll have to call Mr Burke.

It's not what *I* had in mind.

"Now?" I ask, surprised.

"Now," he says. He turns on the light and pulls off my covers.

"I'm not going to," I say.

But I do it. I call Mr Burke, probably waking him up, and I tell him exactly what happened, even that I decided to cheat the night before the test. He says I'll come in on Saturday to take another test, which is okay with me, and I thank him a lot for being so understanding. He's not friendly but he's not absolutely mean either.

"Today I thought I was turning into a criminal," I tell my father when he turns out my light.

Sometimes my father kisses me goodnight and sometimes he doesn't. I never know. But tonight he does.

Riddles in Rhyme

Without a bridle or a saddle,
Across a thing I ride and straddle,
And those I ride, by the help of me,
Though almost blind are made to see.

What force and strength cannot get through
I with a gentle touch can do;
And many in the streets would stand,
Were I not as a friend at hand.

To cross the water I'm the way,
For water I'm above:
I touch it not, and, truth to say,
I neither swim nor move.

In marble walls as white as milk,
Lined with a skin as soft as silk;
Within a fountain crystal clear,
A golden apple does appear.
No doors there are to this stronghold,
Yet thieves break in and steal the gold.

Thirty white horses on a red hill,
    First they champ,
    Then they stamp,
Then they stand still.

Anon

Jelly on the Plate

Jelly on the plate
jelly on the plate
wibble wobble
wibble wobble
jelly on the plate.

Sausage in the pan
sausage in the pan
sizzle sizzle
sizzle sizzle
sausage in the pan.

Sweeties in the jar
sweeties in the jar
pick them out
eat them up
sweeties in the jar.

Burglar in the house
burglar in the house
chuck him out
chuck him out
burglar in the house.

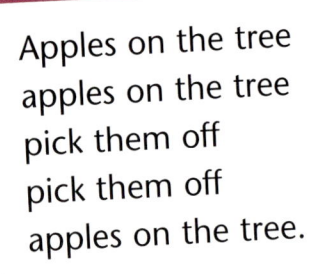

Apples on the tree
apples on the tree
pick them off
pick them off
apples on the tree.

Baby on the floor
baby on the floor
pick it up
pick it up
baby on the floor.

Ants in your pants
ants in your pants
scratch them off
scratch them off
ants in your pants.

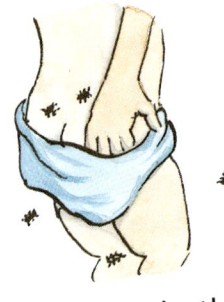

Ice cream in the fridge
ice cream in the fridge
FREEZE!

Anon

BED!

When it is time to go to bed my mum says:
"BED!"
I say:
"Please can I stay up until this film finishes?"
"What time does it finish?" my mum says.
"Ten o'clock," I say.
"No way," my mum says.
"Oh can't I stay up for five minutes?"
"NO."
"Please."
"NO!"
"Oh . . . can't I read in bed?"
"NO!"
"Please."
"Come here, girl . . . You are getting on my nerves
if you are not in that bed
by the time I count to . . ."

I walk slowly up the stairs
my brother is laughing away.
Then my mum starts shouting again.
This time at my brother.

Joni Akinrele

Haiku

I like poetry,
Words chosen carefully and
Arranged on a page.

My dad had a cap;
It was flat, checked, greyey/blue.
I can see it now.

My mum's hair is white;
Her skin is lined and wrinkled.
But her smile still shines.

Margaret Stillie

Centipede's Song

"I've eaten many strange and scrumptious dishes in
    my time,
Like jellied gnats and dandyprats and earwigs
    cooked in slime,
And mice with rice – they're really nice
When roasted in their prime.
(But don't forget to sprinkle them with just a pinch
    of grime.)

"I've eaten fresh mudburgers by the greatest cooks there are,
And scrambled dregs and stinkbug's eggs and hornets stewed in tar,
And pails of snails and lizards' tails,
And beetles by the jar.
(A beetle is improved by just a splash of vinegar.)

"I often eat boiled slobbages. They're grand when served beside
Minced doodlebugs and curried slugs. And have you ever tried
Mosquitoes' toes and wampfish roes
Most delicately fried?
(The only trouble is they disagree with my inside.)

"I'm mad for crispy wasp-stings on a piece of buttered toast,
And pickled spines of porcupines. And then a gorgeous roast
Of dragon's flesh, well hung, not fresh –
It costs a pound at most,
(And comes to you in barrels if you order it by post.)

"I crave the tasty tentacles of octopi for tea
I like hot-dogs, I LOVE hot-frogs, and surely you'll agree
A plate of soil with engine oil's
A super recipe

(I hardly need to mention that it's practically free.)

"For dinner on my birthday shall I tell you what I
    chose:
Hot noodles made from poodles on a slice of garden
    hose –
And a rather smelly jelly
Made of armadillo's toes.
(The jelly is delicious, but you have to hold your
    nose.)

"Now comes," *the Centipede declared,* "the burden
    of my speech:
These foods are rare beyond compare – some are
    right out of reach;
But there's no doubt I'd go without
A million plates of each
For one small mite,
One tiny bite
Of this FANTASTIC PEACH!"

Roald Dahl

WHY?

Why do nettles sting Dad?
Why is the sky blue?
Why do giraffes have such long necks?
I only wish I knew.

Why must I go to bed early?
Why can't I eat lots of sweets?
Why do I have to tidy and wash?
Why can't I have more treats?

Why's your face all scratchy Dad?
Why's Granny got that funny smell?
Why do you call Auntie a battleaxe?
And why does the baby yell?

Why do I have to play quietly?
Why can't I just watch the telly?
Why can't I leave my clothes strewn about?
And only wash when I'm smelly?

Why don't you answer my questions Dad?
Why can't you give them a try?
What do you mean "It's time for bed"?
Why can't you just tell me WHY?

Marcus Lewis

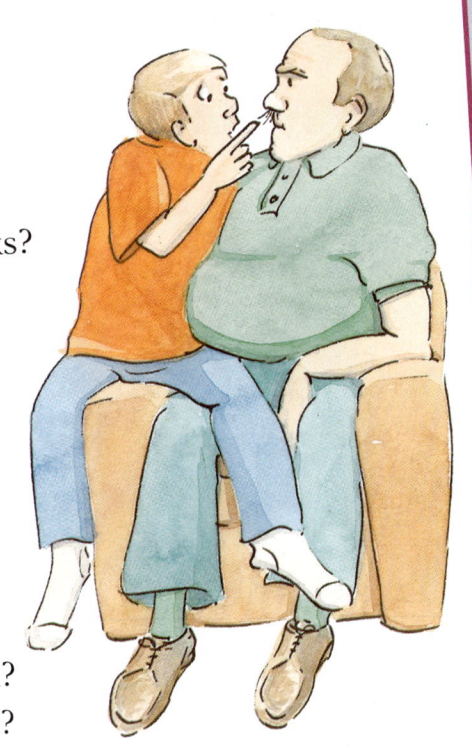

Hey, Danny!

by Robin Klein

"Right," said Danny's mother sternly. "That school bag cost ten pounds. You can just save up your pocket money to buy another one. How could you possibly lose a big school bag, anyhow?"

"Dunno," said Danny. "I just bunged in some empty bottles to take back to the milkbar, and I was sort of swinging it round by the handles coming home, and it sort of fell over that culvert thing down on to a lorry on the motorway."

"And you forgot to write your name and phone number in it as I told you to," said Mrs Hillerey. "Well, you'll just have to use my blue weekend bag till you save up enough pocket money to replace the old one. And no arguments!"

Danny went and got the blue bag from the hall cupboard and looked at it.

The bag was not just blue; it was a vivid, clear, electric blue, like a flash of lightning. The regulation colour for schoolbags at his school was a khaki-olive-brown, inside and out, which didn't show stains from when your can of Coke leaked, or when you left your salami sandwiches uneaten and forgot about them for a month.

"I can't take this bag to school," said Danny. "Not one this colour. Can't I take my books and stuff in one of those green plastic rubbish bags?"

"Certainly not!" said Mrs Hillerey.

On Monday at the bus stop, the kids all stared at the blue bag.

"Hey," said Jim, who was supposed to be his mate. "That looks like one of those bags girls take to ballet classes."

"Hey, Danny, you got one of those frilly dresses in there?" asked Spike.

"Aw, belt up, can't you?" said Danny miserably. On the bus the stirring increased as more and more kids got on. It was a very long trip for Danny. It actually took only twenty minutes – when you had an ordinary brown schoolbag and not a great hunk of sky to carry round with you. Every time anyone spoke to him they called him "Little Boy Blue".

"It matches his lovely blue eyes," said one kid.

"Maybe he's got a little blue trike with training wheels too," said another kid.

"Hey, Danny, why didn't you wear some nice blue ribbons in your hair?"

When Danny got off the bus he made a dash for his classroom and shoved the bag under his desk. First period they had Miss Reynolds, and when she was marking the register she looked along the aisle and saw Danny's bag and said, "That's a very elegant bag you have there, Danny."

Everyone else looked round and saw the blue bag and began carrying on. Danny kept a dignified silence, and after five minutes Miss Reynolds made them stop singing "A life on the Ocean Waves". But all through maths and English, heads kept turning round to grin at Danny and his radiantly blue bag.

At break he sneaked into the art room and mixed poster paints into a shade of khaki-olive-brown which he rubbed over his bag with his hankie.

When the bell rang he had a grey handkerchief, but the bag was still a clear and innocent blue. "Darn thing," Danny muttered in disgust. "Must be made of some kind of special waterproof atomic material. Nothing sticks to it."

"What are you doing in the art room, Daniel?" asked Miss Reynolds. "And what is that terrible painty mess?"

"I was just painting a Zodiac sign on my bag," said Danny.

"I wish you boys wouldn't write things all over your good school bags. Clean up that mess, Danny, and go to your next lesson."

But Danny said he was feeling sick and could he please lie down in the sick bay for a while. He sneaked his blue bag in with him, and found the key to the first-aid box and looked inside for something that would turn bright blue bags brown. There was a little bottle of brown lotion, so Danny tipped the whole lot on to cotton wool and scrubbed it into the surface of the bag. But the lotion just ran off the bag and went all over his hands and the bench top in the sick bay.

"Danny Hillerey!" said the school secretary. "You know very well that no pupil is allowed to unlock the first-aid box. What on earth are you doing?"

"Sorry," said Danny. "Just looking for some liver salts."

"I think you'd better sit quietly out in the fresh air if you feel sick," Mrs Adams said suspiciously. "And who owns that peculiar-looking blue bag?"

"It belongs in the sports equipment shed," said Danny. "It's got measuring tapes and stuff in it. Blue's our house colour."

He went and sat outside with the bag shoved under the seat and looked at it and despaired. Kids from his class started going down to the oval for games, and they started in on him again.

Danny glared and said "Get lost" and "Drop dead". Then Miss Reynolds came along and made him go down to the oval with the others.

On the way there Danny sloshed the blue bag in a puddle of mud – but nothing happened, the blue became shinier, if anything. He also tried grass stains under the sprinkler, which had the same effect. Amongst the line-up of khaki-olive-brown bags, his blue one was as conspicuous as a Clydesdale horse in a herd of small ponies.

"Hey, Danny, what time's your tap dancing lesson?" said the kids.

"Hey, Danny, where did you get that knitting bag? I want to buy one for my aunty."

"Hey, Danny, when did you join the Bluebell marching girls' squad?"

Finally Danny had had enough.

"This bag's very valuable, if you want to know," he said.

"Rubbish," everyone scoffed. "It's just an ordinary old vinyl bag."

"I had to beg my mum to let me bring that bag to school," said Danny. "It took some doing, I can tell you. Usually she won't let it out of the house."

"Why?" demanded everyone. "What's so special about it?"

Danny grabbed his bag and wiped off the traces of mud and poster paint and brown lotion and grass stains. The bag was stained inside where all that had seeped in through the seams and the zip, and it would take some explaining when his mother noticed it. (Which she would, next time she went to spend the weekend at Grandma's.) There was her name inside, E. Hillerey, in big neat letters. E for Enid.

"Well," said Danny, "that bag belonged to . . . well, if you really want to know, it went along on that expedition up Mount Everest."

Everyone jeered.

"It did so," said Danny. "Look, Sir Edmund Hillary, there's his name printed right there inside. And there's a reason it's this funny colour. So it wouldn't get lost in the snow. It was the bag Sir Edmund Hillary carried that flag in they stuck up on top of Mount Everest. But I'm not going to bring it to school any more if all you can do is poke fun at the colour."

Everyone went all quiet and respectful.

"Wow," said Jeff in an awed voice, and he touched the letters that Danny's mother had written with a laundry marking pencil.

"Gosh," said Mark. "We never knew you were related to that Sir Edmund Hillary."

Danny looked modest. "We're only distantly related," he admitted. "He's my dad's second cousin."

"Hey, Danny, can I hold it on the bus? I'll be really careful with it."

"Hey, Danny, can I have a turn when you bring it to school tomorrow?"

"I'll charge you ten pence a go," said Danny.

"That's fair, for a bag that went up to the top of Mount Everest."

"Ten pence a kid," he calculated. "One hundred kids at ten pence a turn, ten pounds. A new brown school bag. And with a bit of luck, I'll earn all that before someone checks up in the library and finds out Sir Edmund Hillary's name's spelt differently!"

Term 3 | Unit 5

I Did a Bad Thing Once

I did a bad thing once.
I took this money from my mother's purse
For bubble gum.
What made it worse,
She bought me some
For being good, while I'd been vice versa
So to speak – that made it worser.

Allan Ahlberg

In the Playground

In the playground
Some run round
Chasing a ball
Or chasing each other;
Some pretend to be
Someone on TV;
Some walk
And talk,
Some stand
On their hands
Against the wall
And some do nothing at all.

Stanley Cook

The Gang

1st boy: Who wants to be in my gang?
2nd boy: Who else have you got?
1st boy: Well really just me at the moment.
2nd boy: That's not a lot.

2nd boy: Who wants to be in his gang?
3rd boy: I do – me!
2nd boy: Right, he's boss, I'm second-in-command,
            You're number three.

3rd boy: Who wants to be in our gang?
            Line up at the den.
            We've got the three leaders already,
            We need a few men.

1st boy: Who wants to be in their gang?
            Don't spread it about.
            I've stopped being boss of it now.
            They voted me out.

1st boy: Who wants to be in my gang?

Allan Ahlberg

Sometimes God

Sometimes when I'm in trouble,
Like if Gary Hubble
And his gang
Are going to get me and beat me up,
Or I'm outside Mr Baggot's door
Waiting to have the slipper for pouring
Paint water in Glenis Parker's shoe,
This is what I do:
I ask for help from God.

Get me out of this, God,
I say.
I'll behave myself, then –
Every day.

Sometimes when I'm really
Scared, like once when I nearly
Got bit by this horse.
Or the other
Week when Russell Tucker's brother
Was going to beat me up
For throwing Russell Tucker's P.E. bag
On the boiler-house roof, or Roy
And me got caught in the toilets
By Mr Baggot turning all the taps on
And he said,
I've had enough of boys like you,

This is what I do:
I ask for help from God.

Stop this happening, God,
I say.
I'll believe in You then –
Every day.

And it works . . . sometimes.

Allan Ahlberg

My Gerbil

My gerbil sulks when I go out.
I promise you it's true,
I know that's what he's doing
For I often do it too.
He sits there with his back to me,
And makes me feel so cruel.
I have explained, so he must know
I have to go to school.

I think he knows me very well,
Can even read my mind.
I just hate going off to school
And leaving him behind.
"He'll sleep," says Mum,
    "That's what he does
When we are out all day."
But I worry just in case he wakes
And needs me there to play.

I hurry up the garden path,
I'm listening for the sound
His squeaky tread-wheel always makes
As he goes round and round.
It's very quiet today, I think
Mum must have oiled that wheel.
Then suddenly I realise.
I can't say what I feel.

I feel the tears roll down my cheeks.
Surprisingly, I find
My sister, though she teases me
Is also very kind.
I'll miss my gerbil very much,

He was my special friend.
My Mum says I'll get over it
But broken hearts don't mend.

Beatrice Higgins

Limericks

I'd rather have fingers than toes;
I'd rather have ears than a nose;
    And as for my hair,
    I'm glad that it's there.
I'll be awfully sad when it goes.

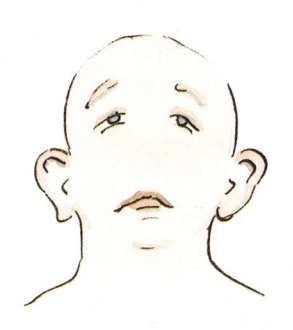

Gelett Burgess

There was an old poacher called Bruce
Whose belt was always too loose.
    One day in the town
    His trousers fell down,
And out came three cats and a goose.

Michael Palin

Eddie and the Gerbils

Not long ago
we went on holiday with some people
who've got gerbils.
We haven't got any pets
and Eddie (he was two years old)
he thought they were
WONDERFUL.
He was always looking in their cage
going,
"Hallo gerbils, hallo gerbils, hallo gerbils."
And when the boys took them out of the cage
Eddie loved stroking them,
going,
"Hallo gerbils, hallo gerbils, hallo gerbils,"
all over again.
Now,
when we got home from the holiday
Like I said,
we haven't got any pets.
What we've got, is
MICE.
So we wanted to get rid of them.
So we rang up the council to ask for the mouse-man

to come over and get rid of them.
The mouse-man.
That's not a man who is a mouse.
Silly,
it's a man who comes over
and he goes round
sniffing along the walls
and behind cupboards
to find where the mice go.
Then he puts down these little trays of poison,
only the mice don't know it's poison,
they think it's some really nice stuff
like biscuits.
And this poison
it burns them up from the inside
And they just die.
The dead ones pong a bit.
The bloke puts down little trays of this poison
and the mice find it and go,
"Wow. This looks really tasty stuff,"
gobble gobble gobble
clunk. Dead.
gobble gobble gobble
clunk.
So one morning we're having breakfast
and when Eddie has breakfast
sometimes he sits at the table
sometimes he sits on the table
sometimes he sits under the table.
Well,

this particular morning
he was sitting under the table.
So I'm eating my breakfast
munch munch munch
and suddenly I hear
"Hallo gerbils."
"Uh?" Ignore it. Munch munch munch.
"Hallo gerbils."
Better have a look.
Oh no.
He's got a dead mouse in his hand.
Clutching it,
Head poking out the top of his fist
tail out the bottom.
And he's stroking it.
The dead mouse.
And he's going,
"Hallo gerbils hallo gerbils hallo gerbils."

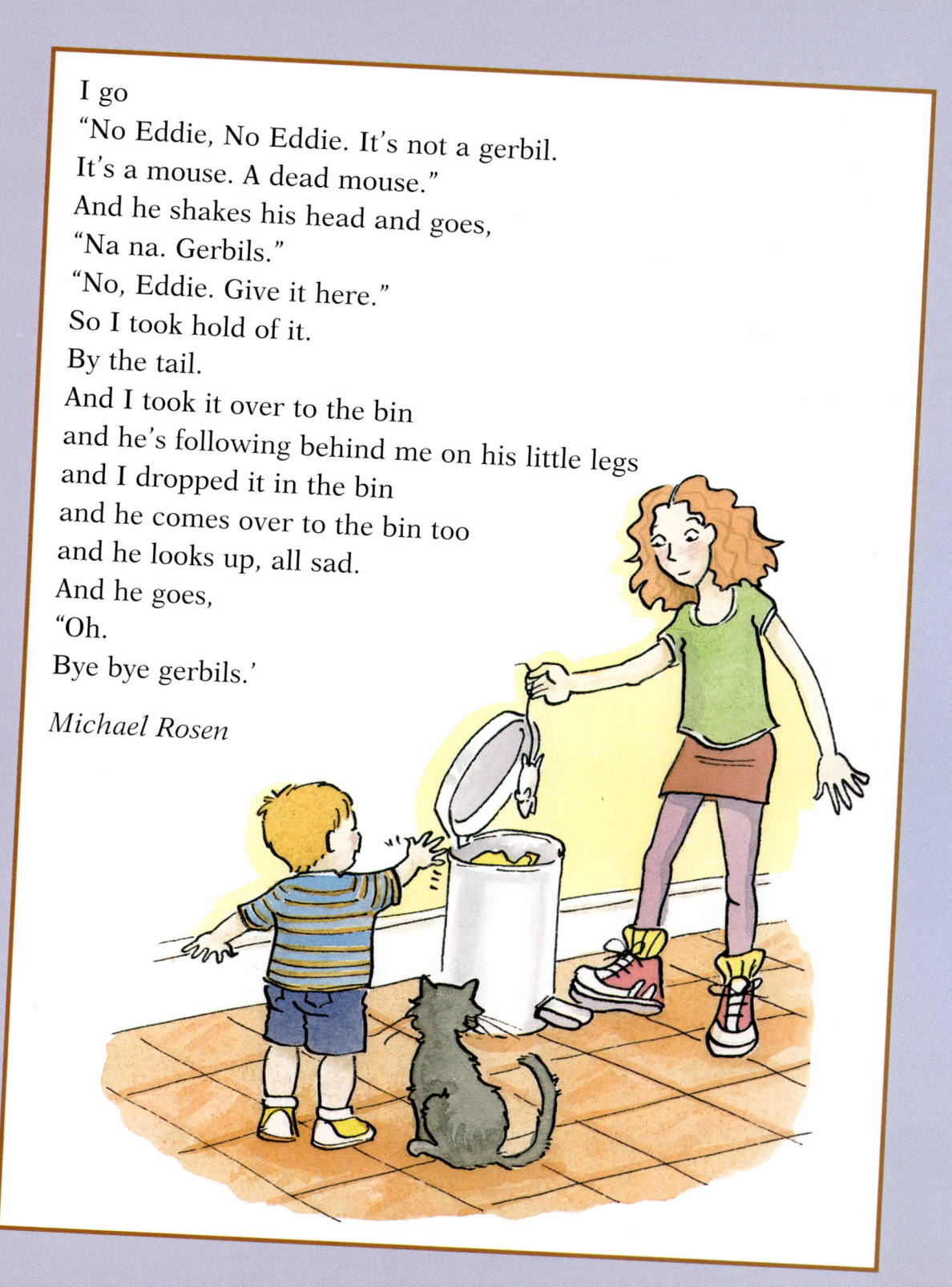

I go
"No Eddie, No Eddie. It's not a gerbil.
It's a mouse. A dead mouse."
And he shakes his head and goes,
"Na na. Gerbils."
"No, Eddie. Give it here."
So I took hold of it.
By the tail.
And I took it over to the bin
and he's following behind me on his little legs
and I dropped it in the bin
and he comes over to the bin too
and he looks up, all sad.
And he goes,
"Oh.
Bye bye gerbils.'

Michael Rosen

Lost – One Pair of Legs
by Joan Aiken

Once there was a vain, proud, careless, thoughtless boy called Cal Finhorn, who was very good at tennis. He won this game, he won that game, he won this match, he won that match, and then he won a tournament, and had a silver cup with his name on it.

Winning this cup made him even prouder – too proud to speak to any of the other players at the tournament. As soon as he could, he took his silver cup and hurried away to the entrance of the sports ground, where the buses stop.

"Just wait till I show them this cup at home," he was thinking. "I'll make Jenny polish it every day."

Jenny was Cal's younger sister. He made her do lots of things for him – wash his cereal bowl, make his bed, clean his shoes, feed his rabbits.

He had not allowed her to come to the tournament, in case he lost.

On the way across the grass towards the bus stop, Cal saw a great velvety fluttering butterfly with purple and white and black circles on its wings.

Cal was a boy who acted before he thought. Maybe sometimes he didn't think at all. He hit the butterfly a smack with his tennis racket, and it fell to the ground stunned. Cal felt sorry then, perhaps, for what he had done to it, but it was too late, for he heard a tremendous clap of thunder, and then he saw the Lady Esclairmonde, the queen of winged things, hovering right in his path. She looked very frightening indeed – she was all wrapped in a cloak of grey and white feathers, she had the face of a hawk, hands like claws, a crest of flame, and her hair and ribbons and the train of her dress flew out sideways, as if a Force Twelve gale surrounded her. Cal could hear a fluttering sound, such as a flag or sail makes in a high wind. His own heart was fluttering inside him; he could hear that too, like a lark inside a biscuit tin.

"Why did you hit my butterfly, Cal?" asked the Lady Esclairmonde.

Cal tried to brazen it out. He grinned at the lady. But he glanced nervously round him, wondering if people noticed that she was speaking to him. Perhaps, he thought hopefully, they might think she was congratulating him on his silver cup.

Nobody else seemed to have noticed the lady.

"Ah, shucks, it was only a silly butterfly," said Cal. "Anyway I don't suppose I hurt it."

"Oh," said the lady. "What makes you think that?"

"It hasn't written me a letter of complaint," said Cal, grinning.

As he spoke these words he noticed a very odd feeling under his right hip. And when he looked down, he saw his right leg remove itself from him, and go hopping off across the grass, heel and toe, heel and toe, as if it were dancing a hornpipe. The leg seemed delighted to be off and away on its own. It went dancing over to the bus stop. Just then a number 19 bus swept in to the stop, and the leg hopped up on board and was borne away.

"*Hey!*" bawled Cal in horror. "Come back! Come back! You're my leg! You've no right to go off and leave me in the lurch. And that isn't the right bus!"

Lurch was the right word. With only one leg, Cal was swaying about like a hollyhock in a gale. He was obliged to prop himself up with his tennis racket. He turned angrily to the lady and said, "Did *you* do that? You've no right to take away my leg! It isn't fair!"

"Nothing is fair," said the lady sternly. "What you did to my butterfly was not fair either. You may think yourself lucky I didn't take the other leg as well."

"I think you are a mean old witch!" said Cal.

Instantly he felt a jerk as his left leg undid itself from the hip. Cal bumped down on the grass, hard, while his left leg went capering away across the grass, free as you please, up on the point of its toe, pirouetting like a ballerina. When it reached the bus stop a number 16 had just pulled up; the left leg hopped nimbly on board and was carried away.

"You're on the wrong bus! Come back!" shouted Cal, but the leg made no answer to that.

Tod Crossfinch, who was in Cal's class at school, came by just then.

"Coo! Cal," he said, "you lost your legs, then?"

"You can blooming well see I have!" said Cal angrily.

"Want me to wheel you to the bus stop in my bike basket?" said Tod.

"No! I want my legs back," said Cal.

"You won't get them back," the Lady Esclairmonde told him, "until a pair of butterflies brings them."

Then she vanished in a flash of lightning and smell of burnt feathers.

"Ooh, Cal," said Jenny, "what*ever* have you done with your legs?"

"They ran off and left me," said Cal, very annoyed that he had to keep telling people that his legs didn't want to stay with him.

As Cal spoke, all the butterflies rose up in a cloud of wings and flew away.

"Oh, poor Cal!" said Jenny. "Never mind, I'll wheel you about in my doll's pushchair."

"I'd rather wheel myself about on your skateboard," said Cal.

Jenny was rather disappointed, but she kindly let him have the skateboard.

"Er, Jenny," said Cal, "you don't suppose your butterflies would bring back my legs, do you?"

"Oh, no, Cal," said Jenny. "Why should they? You haven't

done anything for them. In fact they don't like you much, because you always chase them and try to catch them in your handkerchief."

Cal's father said that Cal had better try advertising to get his legs back.

So he put a card in the post office window, and also a notice in the local paper:

LOST

One pair of legs. Reward offered.

Lots and lots of people turned up hoping for the reward, but the legs they brought were never the right ones. There were old, rheumatic legs in wrinkled boots, or skinny girls' legs in knitted leg warmers, or babies' legs or football legs or ballet dancers' legs in pink cotton slippers.

"I never knew before that so many legs ran away from their owners," said Jenny.

This fact ought to have cheered Cal up a bit, but it didn't.

Jenny would have liked to adopt a pair of the ballet legs, but her mother said no, a canary and some rabbits were all the pets they had room for. "Besides, those legs must belong to someone else who wants them back."

Then a friend told Cal's father that one of Cal's legs was performing every night in the local pub, the Ring o' Roses. "Dances around the bar, very active, it does. Brings in a whole lot o' custom."

Mr Finhorn went along one night to see, and sure enough he recognized Cal's leg, with the scar on the knee where he had fallen down the front steps carrying a bottle of milk. But when the leg saw Mr Finhorn it danced away along the bar, and skipped out of the window, and went hopping off down the road in the dark.

The other leg was heard of up in London; it had got a job at the Hippodrome Theatre, dancing on the stage with a parasol tucked into its garter.

"I don't believe they'll *ever* come back to me now," said Cal hopelessly.

Cal was becoming very sad and quiet, not a bit like what he had been before. He was a good deal nicer to Jenny and even helped his mother with the dishwashing, balancing on a kitchen stool.

"It's not very likely," his mother agreed. "Not now they're used to earning their own living."

"Maybe if you fed my butterflies every day, they'd bring your legs back," suggested Jenny.

So Cal rolled out on his skateboard every day and fed the butterflies with handfuls of sugar. They grew quite accustomed to him, and would perch on his arms and head and hands.

But summer was nearly over; autumn was coming; there were fewer butterflies every day. And still Cal's legs did not come back.

School began again. Every day Cal went to school on the

skateboard, rolling himself along with his hands. He couldn't play football, because of having no legs, but he could still swim, so he did that three times a week, in the school pool.

One day while he was swimming he saw two butterflies floating in the centre of the pool. They were flapping and struggling a little, but very feebly; it looked as if they were going to drown.

Cal dog-paddled towards them, as fast as he could. "Poor things," he thought, "they must feel horrible with their wings all wet and floppy."

They were two of a kind he had never seen before – very large, silvery in colour, with lavender streaks and long trailing points to their wings.

Cal wondered how he could save them.

"For if I take them in my hands," he thought, "I might

squash them. And they would have to go under water when I swim. Oh, if only I had my legs! Then I could swim with my legs and hold the butterflies above water."

But he hadn't got his legs, so he could only swim with his arms.

"I'll have to take the butterflies in my mouth," Cal thought then.

He didn't much care for the idea. In fact it made him shivery down his back – to think of having two live, fluttery butterflies inside his mouth. Still, that seemed the only way to save them. He opened his mouth very wide indeed – luckily it was a big one anyway – and gently scooped the two butterflies in with his tongue, as they themselves scoop in sugar. He was careful to take in as little water as possible.

Then, with open mouth and head well above water, he swam like mad for the side of the pool.

But, on the way, the butterflies began to fidget and flutter inside his mouth.

"Oh, I can't bear it," thought Cal.

Now the butterflies were beating and battering inside his mouth – he felt as if his head were hollow, and the whole of it were filled with great flapping wings and kicking legs and waving whiskers. They tickled and rustled and scraped and scrabbled and nearly drove him frantic. Still he went on swimming as fast as he was able.

Then it got so bad that he felt as if his whole head was going to be lifted off. But it was not only his head – suddenly Cal, head, arms, and all, found himself lifted right out of the swimming pool and carried through the air by the two butterflies whirring like helicopters inside his mouth.

They carried him away from the school and back to his own garden, full of lavender and nasturtiums and Michaelmas daisies, where Jenny was scattering sugar on a tray.

And there, sitting in a deckchair waiting for him, were his own two legs!

Cal opened his mouth so wide in amazement that the two silvery butterflies shot out, and dropped down on to the tray to refresh themselves with a little sugar. Which they must have needed, after carrying Cal all wet and dripping.

And Cal's legs stood up, stretched themselves a bit, in a carefree way, heel and toe, the way cats do, then came hopping over to hook themselves on to Cal's hips, as calm and friendly as if they had never been away.

Was Cal a different boy after that? He was indeed. For one thing, those legs had learned such a lot, while they were off on their own, that he could have made an easy living in any circus, or football team, or dance company – and did, for a while, when he grew up.

Also, he never grew tired of listening to his legs, who used to argue in bed, every night, recalling the days when they had been off in the world by themselves.

". . . That time when I jumped into the tiger's cage . . ."

"Shucks! That wasn't so extra brave. Not like when I tripped up the bank robbers . . ."

"That was nothing."

"You weren't there. You don't know how it happened!"

So they used to argue.

For the rest of his life Cal was very polite to his legs, in case they ever took a fancy to go off on holiday again.

A Necklace of Raindrops

by Joan Aiken

A man called Mr Jones and his wife lived near the sea. One stormy night Mr Jones was in his garden when he saw the holly tree by his gate begin to toss and shake.

A voice cried, "Help me! I'm stuck in the tree! Help me, or the storm will go on all night."

Very surprised, Mr Jones walked down to the tree. In the middle of it was a tall man with a long grey cloak, and a long grey beard, and the brightest eyes you ever saw.

"Who are you?" Mr Jones said. "What are you doing in my holly tree?"

"I got stuck in it, can't you see? Help me out, or the storm will go on all night. I am the North Wind, and it is my job to blow the storm away."

So Mr Jones helped the North Wind out of the holly tree. The North Wind's hands were as cold as ice.

"Thank you," said the North Wind. "My cloak is torn, but never mind. You have helped me, so now I will do something for you."

"I don't need anything," Mr Jones said. "My wife and I have a baby girl, just born, and we are as happy as any two people in the world."

"In that case," said the North Wind, "I will be the baby's

godfather. My birthday present to her will be this necklace of raindrops."

From under his grey cloak he pulled out a fine, fine silver chain. On the chain were three bright, shining drops.

"You must put it round the baby's neck," he said. "The raindrops will not wet her, and they will not come off. Every year, on her birthday, I will bring her another drop. When she has four drops she will stay dry, even if she goes out in the hardest rainstorm. And when she has five drops no thunder or lightning can harm her. And when she has six drops she will not be blown away, even by the strongest wind. And when she has seven raindrops she will be able to swim the deepest river. And when she has eight raindrops she will be able to swim the widest sea. And when she has nine raindrops she will be able to make the rain stop raining if she claps her hands. And when she has ten raindrops she will be able to make it start raining if she blows her nose."

"Stop, stop!" cried Mr Jones. "That is quite enough for one little girl!"

"I was going to stop anyway," said the North Wind. "Mind, she must never take the chain off, or it might bring bad luck. I must be off, now, to blow away the storm. I shall be back on her next birthday, with the fourth raindrop."

And he flew away up into the sky, pushing the clouds before him so that the moon and stars could shine out.

Mr Jones went into his house and put the chain with the

Term 3 | Unit 8

three raindrops round the neck of the baby, who was called Laura.

A year soon went by, and when the North Wind came back to the little house by the sea, Laura was able to crawl about, and to play with her three bright, shining raindrops. But she never took the chain off.

When the North Wind had given Laura her fourth raindrop she could not get wet, even if she was out in the hardest rain. Her mother would put her out in the garden in her pram, and people passing on the road would say, "Look at that poor little baby, left out in all this rain. She will catch cold!"

But little Laura was quite dry, and quite happy, playing with the raindrops and waving to her godfather the North Wind as he flew over.

Next year he brought her her fifth raindrop. And the year after that, the sixth. And the year after that, the seventh. Now Laura could not be harmed by the worst storm, and if she fell into a pond or river she floated like a feather. And when she had eight raindrops she was able to swim across the widest sea – but as she was happy at home she had never tried.

206

And when she had nine raindrops Laura found that she could make the rain stop, by clapping her hands. So there were many, many sunny days by the sea. But Laura did not always clap her hands when it rained, for she loved to see the silver drops come sliding out of the sky.

Now it was time for Laura to go to school. You can guess how the other children loved her! They would call, "Laura, Laura, make it stop raining, please, so that we can go out to play."

And Laura always made the rain stop for them.

But there was a girl called Meg who said to herself, "It isn't fair. Why should Laura have that lovely necklace and be able to stop the rain? Why shouldn't I have it?"

So Meg went to the teacher and said, "Laura is wearing a necklace."

Then the teacher said to Laura, "You must take the necklace off in school, dear. That is the rule."

"But it will bring bad luck if I take it off," said Laura.

"Of course it will not bring bad luck. I will put it in a box for you and keep it safe till after school."

So the teacher put the necklace in a box.

But Meg saw where she put it. And when the children were out playing, and the teacher was having her dinner, Meg went quickly and took the necklace and put it in her pocket.

When the teacher found that the necklace was gone, she was very angry and sad.

"Who has taken Laura's necklace?" she asked.

But nobody answered.

Meg kept her hand tight in her pocket, holding the necklace.

And poor Laura cried all the way home. Her tears rolled down her cheeks like rain as she walked along by the sea.

"Oh," she cried, "what will happen when I tell my godfather that I have lost his present?"

A fish put his head out of the water and said, "Don't cry, Laura dear. You put me back in the sea when a wave threw me on the sand. I will help you find your necklace."

And a bird flew down and called, "Don't cry, Laura dear. You saved me when a storm blew me on to your roof and hurt my wing. I will help you find your necklace."

And a mouse popped his head out of a hole and said, "Don't cry, Laura dear. You saved me once when I fell in the river. I will help you find your necklace."

So Laura dried her eyes. "How will you help me?" she asked.

"I will look under the sea," said the fish. "And I will ask my brothers to help me."

"I will fly about and look in the fields and woods and roads," said the bird. "And I will ask all my brothers to help me."

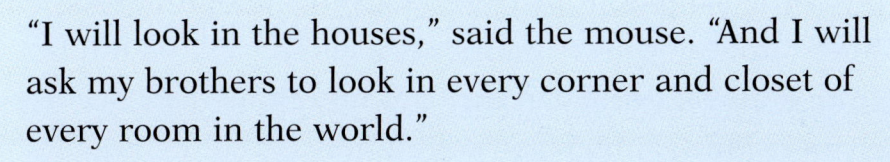

"I will look in the houses," said the mouse. "And I will ask my brothers to look in every corner and closet of every room in the world."

So they set to work.

While Laura was talking to her three friends, what was Meg doing?

She put on the necklace and walked out in a rainstorm. But the rain made her very wet! And when she clapped her hands to stop it raining, the rain took no notice. It rained harder than ever.

The necklace would only work for its true owner.

So Meg was angry. But she still wore the necklace, until her father saw her with it on.

"Where did you get that necklace?" he asked.

"I found it in the road," Meg said. Which was not true!

"It is too good for a child," her father said. And he took it away from her. Meg and her father did not know that a little mouse could see them from a hole in the wall.

The mouse ran to tell his friends that the necklace was in Meg's house. And ten more mice came back with him to drag it away. But when they got there, the necklace was gone. Meg's father had sold it, for a great deal of money, to a silversmith. Two days later, a little mouse saw it in the silversmith's shop, and ran to tell his friends. But before the mice could come to take it, the silversmith had sold it to a trader who was buying fine and rare presents for the birthday of the Princess of Arabia.

Then a bird saw the necklace and flew to tell Laura.

"The necklace is on a ship, which is sailing across the sea to Arabia."

"We will follow the ship," said the fishes. "We will tell you which way it goes. Follow us!"

But Laura stood on the edge of the sea.

"How can I swim all that way without my necklace?" she cried.

"I will take you on my back," said a dolphin. "You have often thrown me good things to eat when I was hungry."

So the dolphin took her on his back, and the fishes went on in front, and the birds flew above, and after many days they came to Arabia.

"Now where is the necklace?" called the fishes to the birds.

"The King of Arabia has it. He is going to give it to the Princess for her birthday tomorrow."

"Tomorrow is my birthday too," said Laura. "Oh, what will my godfather say when he comes to give me my tenth raindrop and finds that I have not got the necklace?"

The birds led Laura into the King's garden. And she slept all night under a palm tree. The grass was all dry, and the flowers were all brown, because it was so hot, and had not rained for a year.

Next morning the Princess came into the garden to open her presents. She had many lovely things: a flower that could sing, and a cage full of birds with green and silver feathers; a book that she could read for ever because it had no last page, and a cat who could play cat's cradle; a silver dress of spiderwebs and a gold dress of goldfish scales; a clock with a real cuckoo to tell the time, and a boat made out of a great pink shell. And among all the other presents was Laura's necklace.

When Laura saw the necklace she ran out from under the palm tree and cried, "Oh, please, that necklace is mine!"

The King of Arabia was angry. "Who is this girl?" he said. "Who let her into my garden? Take her away and drop her in the sea!"

But the Princess, who was small and pretty, said, "Wait a minute, Papa," and to Laura she said, "How do you know it is your necklace?"

"Because my godfather gave it to me! When I am wearing it I can go out in the rain without getting wet, no storm can harm me, I can swim any river and any sea, and I can make the rain stop raining."

"But can you make it start to rain?" said the King.

"Not yet," said Laura. "Not till my godfather gives me the tenth raindrop."

"If you can make it rain you shall have the necklace," said the King. "For we badly need rain in this country."

But Laura was sad because she could not make it rain till she had her tenth raindrop.

Just then the North Wind came flying into the King's garden.

"There you are, god-daughter!" he said. "I have been looking all over the world for you, to give you your birthday present. Where is your necklace?"

"The Princess has it," said poor Laura.

Then the North Wind was angry. "You should not have taken it off!" he said. And he dropped the raindrop on to the dry grass, where it was lost. Then he flew away. Laura started to cry.

"Don't cry," said the kind little Princess. "You shall have the necklace back, for I can see it is yours." And she put the chain over Laura's head. As soon as she did so, one of Laura's tears ran down and hung on the necklace beside the nine raindrops, making ten. Laura started to smile, she dried her eyes and blew her nose. And, guess what! as soon as she blew her nose, the rain began falling! It rained and it rained, the trees all spread out their leaves, and the flowers stretched their petals, they were so happy to have a drink.

At last Laura clapped her hands to stop the rain.

The King of Arabia was very pleased. "That is the finest necklace I have ever seen," he said. "Will you come and stay with us every year, so that we have enough rain?" And Laura said she would do this.

Then they sent her home in the Princess's boat, made out of a pink shell. And the birds flew overhead, and the fishes swam in front.

"I am happy to have my necklace back," said Laura. "But I am even happier to have so many friends."

What happened to Meg? The mice told the North Wind that she had taken Laura's necklace. And he came and blew the roof off her house and let in the rain, so she was SOAKING WET!

The Slave who became Chief

by Charles Mungoshi

Kakore was Chief Chisvo's slave. When still a boy he was captured after a battle in which most of his own people were killed by Chief Chisvo's army. Now he was a full-grown man and he lived in the Chief's guta, herding hundreds of cattle and goats.

Kakore was above the age when most men had wives and children of their own because nobody would offer their daughter to a slave. At first he had thought about escape, but he knew that the Chief's young warriors would soon recapture him. Also, if he did escape, he wouldn't know where to go once he left the guta. He would die of hunger or he might be eaten by the wild beasts living in the thick jungle nearby. Kakore didn't know where any of his people who had survived the battle lived. As he had grown up, his memories slowly faded and now, as a young man, he couldn't clearly remember his mother and father. This made him very sad.

Chief Chisvo was not hard on Kakore, yet he rarely saw him in his everyday life as a herdsman. But the young men of the village, and even some of the children, never let a day go by without reminding him that he was a slave. They made it clear through their words and actions that they could do whatever they liked with him. His life was in their hands. He was not even allowed to look at any of the girls in the guta. The price of being a slave was to live alone without a wife, cook his own food, fetch his own water and firewood, and wash his own clothes.

Kakore lived in a hut near Chief Chisvo's cattle pens. His only companions were his dog, his mbira and the single spear with which he hunted hares and rabbits for his meals. In the evenings, when he had corralled the Chief's cattle and goats, he would sit in his hut playing his mbira and singing the rainmaking songs of his now distant land. The animals were his only audience. They would look at him with their sad eyes and listen to him as they chewed.

But one year a severe drought struck Chief Chisvo's land. First, the wells dried up, then the little streams, then the big rivers and finally the deep hippo and crocodile pools. Then, in the second rainless year, even the trees failed to bring forth new spring leaves. Rocks and boulders in the nearby hills split and set fire to the mountains. The wild game, on which people lived, left the land to search for greener pastures. The only food available was lean meat from the cattle that were dying in their hundreds. But there was still a little water high up in the granite hills where it oozed out in thin rusty trickles from ancient rocks. It took the most agile young warriors and girls a whole day's journey to collect, and people feared that even this little water would soon dry up.

Chief Chisvo's people were, therefore, most surprised to learn that, whenever Kakore came back from the pastures in the evening, he carried a goatskin bag full of cool clear mountain water. This was discovered by some young boys who helped Kakore corral the Chief's cattle and goats. Kakore heard them complaining how thirsty they were and gave them some water from his bag. He told the boys to promise not to tell anyone. But who keeps a slave's word? So the boys had gone home and told their elders who, in turn, told the Chief.

Now Chief Chisvo was an old man and very wise. He told his people to leave the slave alone. If it was the slave's wish that no one should know where he got his drinking water, then the Chief would not interfere with his wish. He said he had experienced calamities worse than hunger befalling whole villages because of foolhardy people who did not respect the customs of others.

But only Chief Chisvo and some of his elders and seasoned warriors had such wisdom. The hot-blooded young men, who had not yet been to battle, knew of nothing that was sacred to a slave. Why, they thought, should he have fresh water to drink in their own land when they did not?

So a few young men of the guta – including some of Chief Chisvo's sons – got together to plan how to make Kakore show them where he had found water. Some suggested that they tie him up and then force him, at the point of a spear, to tell them his secret. But the older ones among them said that if they did this Kakore might prefer to die and then where would they be? After all, they argued, Kakore was a slave, they his enemies, so he might happily go to his death knowing that everyone in the guta would die of thirst and, in this way, his people would be avenged. No, older young men advised, the best plan would be to follow Kakore when he took the animals out to pasture and watch everything he did.

"What happens if he has magic that tells him he's being followed and decides not to go to the water?" some of the more impatient young men asked.

"In that case," the older ones replied, "we will watch him day and night. Sooner or later he will feel that he needs a drink. That will be our moment." The young men had thought this was a slow way of doing things but they had been taught not to argue with people older than themselves.

As it turned out, it wasn't at all difficult to find out where Kakore got his water from. In fact, Kakore himself seemed not to care whether or not anyone saw him performing his magic. He just drove the cattle and goats straight up into the hills playing his mbira, his dog snapping at the heels of the animals. Once up in the hills, he went a little higher and sat down on a flat rock from where he could watch the grazing animals and have a view of the guta. The young men following Kakore, hiding behind a large boulder, had the biggest surprise of their lives. They saw that he was sitting on a rock but it was the huge musasa tree against which he was leaning that finally drew their attention. The tree seemed to grow straight out of the middle of the rock and it had the greenest leaves they had ever seen. Every other blade of grass, every shrub and bush and tree in the whole land was tinder dry, yet here was a huge tree in full bloom! There were even rain-birds singing and twittering in its thick foliage!

The young men's previous courage deserted them. They felt they were in the presence of a power much stronger than themselves, or their Chief or the strongest of the Chief's n'angas. The way the slave sat leaning against the tree as if he owned it! Not only that, but the way he moved his head, scanning the lands below him as if everything were in his hands.

The young men felt helpless watching Kakore, as if they were in the grip of a supernatural power. They couldn't retreat because they felt that the slightest noise would reach the ears of the man under the tree. They weren't even sure whether he was a man or an ancestral spirit. So they stayed rooted behind the boulder, breathing very lightly, as they were afraid that Kakore might hear them.

Then they heard strains of the most haunting mbira music in the world. It was as if the earth had opened and released all its spirits to roam the land freely. The young men trembled. They knew, without doubt, that they were witnessing something not meant for them or perhaps for any living being on earth.

Then they realized that Kakore had begun to sing. It wasn't really singing but the kind of noise one would expect to hear from a big tree as its roots are torn out of the ground. Yet they could hear the words clearly,

> "I call upon you, Little Cloud
> Swirl and swell, Little Cloud
> Twirl and spin, Little Cloud
> Let go, Little Cloud, let drop
> Let drop a little dew."

Then it seemed as if the sky shattered and a forked tongue of the whitest flame sprang out of the rock. The whole mountain seemed to explode in a deafening roar which faded over the distant land. Then there was a grumbling as if a lion were behind the next boulder. Suddenly the young men felt heavy blows clubbing their heads and, before they realized that it was raining, they were soaked to the marrow. They didn't even wait to see what happened next. They didn't even discuss whether they should go back home. They were already in their mother's huts, behind bolted doors, when they remembered that the rain had stopped immediately, as soon as they left the hill. The land was as dry as ever before. They felt very ashamed that they had left their spears and clubs and bows and arrows on the hill but they also knew that nothing could persuade them to go back and fetch them.

Back on the hill, when Kakore saw that there was enough water to fill his bag from the hole in the rock at the foot of the tree, he began to chant another song,

> *"Old Chief Sun*
> *Old Chief, hear me*
> *Come out, Old Chief*
> *Burn down, burn all dry*
> *Come now, Old Chief Sun."*

And the sun came out in all its fierceness and drank up every little drop of water that had fallen in the most hidden and sheltered nooks and crannies.

For three days the young men who had followed Kakore up the mountain would not talk, even among themselves, of what they had seen. It seemed as if a strange sickness gripped them. They would neither eat nor speak when spoken to. Their people could not understand what had happened to them. They went to consult the most powerful n'anga of the guta but he couldn't understand what had come over the young men. All he could say was, "They must have seen death."

Every day Kakore took the animals into the hills and brought them down again in the evening carrying his goatskin bag of cool clear water and playing his mbira, seemingly unaware of what had happened in the guta.

Then, early one morning, just before sunrise, Kakore received some very important visitors in his hut, Chief Chisvo himself and his eldest advisors. After they had exchanged greetings, the Chief, without wasting time, said simply, "Help us" and looked at his advisors as if to confirm that he had said the right words. The elders nodded their heads in unison and Kakore understood what they meant.

He took down his goatskin bag from a peg above his stool and had a little drink without saying a word to his visitors. Then he held out the bag and the Chief who received it took a little drink of water. (How he would have loved to take a longer and deeper drink!) In silence the bag was passed to everyone in the room and they all took a sip of cool clear water. When everyone had drunk a little, the bag returned to its owner, the slave.

Kakore now spoke softly and with great sadness. "In my land, among my people, it is the custom to give our visitors a drink of water before any conversation, even before any greetings are made. You may have come a long way without water, and what kind of person would I be if I engaged you in useless talk when you might be drawing your last thirsty breath?" The Chief and his elders nodded their understanding. Then, without another word, Kakore stood up, took his mbira and began to play as he led his guests up the hill . . .

What else is there to say? The moment the Chief and his elders stepped down from the shelter of the big musasa tree they were immediately soaked to the skin.

Back in the guta, Chief Chisvo called a meeting with his advisors, army generals, n'angas and Big Aunts of the Land. No one said anything after the Chief had said what he had to say.

The preparations for the installation of the new Chief were made in a very wet two weeks. It was that kind of quiet but persistent rain that soaks deep into the heart of the earth without turning the top soil into a rock-hard corn-thrashing floor. There was no lightning or thunder but a quiet downpour, soothing to the ear and echoed by the sound of the birds in the hills and crickets and frogs in the flooded plains and overflowing rivers.

In the third week, when the sun came out of the clouds, Chief Chisvo handed over his instruments of chieftainship to Kakore, the former slave and rainmaker. And, since it was the custom of that land that no one should rule the people without a wife, Chief Chisvo himself asked one of his eldest unmarried daughters if she would "help the new Chief run the affairs of the guta."

The feast of the instalment of the new Chief lasted for a whole month. No one, not even the eldest of the elders of the guta, could remember a feast that had lasted so long. But the real surprise was revealed in a remark that one of the Chief's youngest sons made to his father afterwards, "There was so much drinking over so many days and yet not even Musindo and Chikukwa picked a quarrel." He was a hot-tempered young man who had just graduated from herding goats, and there was nothing he liked better than an exchange of blows. He hoped that he would see lots of blood during the feast and felt disappointed that not even the most querulous drunks of the village – Musindo and Chikukwa – had taken advantage of the feast to entertain him to a fist fight.

It was said that in the years that Kakore ruled in Chief Chisvo's land there was never a war. Even more surprisingly, Kakore never seemed to give orders, yet things were always done and he is the best-remembered Chief that ever ruled the land. When Kakore died, he was buried under the musasa tree on the hill and that is where the people go to pray for rain, even today, whenever there is a need.

A Chinese Fairy Tale

Retold by Laurence Houseman

Tiki-Pu was a small grub of a thing; but he had a true love of Art deep down in his soul. There it hung mewing and complaining, struggling to work its way out through the raw exterior that bound it.

Tiki-Pu's master professed to be an artist: he had apprentices and students, who came daily to work under him, and a large studio littered about with the performances of himself and his pupils. On the walls hung also a few real works by the older men, all long since dead.

This studio Tiki-Pu swept; for those who worked in it he ground colours, washed brushes and ran errands, bringing them their dog chops and bird's nest soup from the nearest eating-house whenever they were too busy to go out for it themselves. He himself had to feed mainly on the breadcrumbs which the students screwed into pellets for their drawings and then threw about on the floor. It was on the floor, also, that he had to sleep at night.

Tiki-Pu looked after the blinds, and mended the window-panes, which were often broken when the apprentices threw their brushes and mahl-sticks at him. Also he strained rice-paper over the linen stretchers, ready for the painters to work on; and for a treat, now and then, a lazy one would allow him to mix a colour for him. Then it was that Tiki-Pu's soul came down into his finger tips, and his heart beat so that he gasped for joy. Oh, the yellow and the greens, and the lakes and cobalts, and the purples which sprang from the blending of them! Sometimes it was all he could do to keep himself from crying out.

Tiki-Pu, while he squatted and ground at the colour-powders, would listen to his master lecturing to the students. He knew by heart the names of all the painters and their schools, and the name of the great leader of them all who had lived and passed from their midst more than three hundred years ago; he knew that too, a name like the sound of the wind, Wio-Wani: the big picture at the end of the studio was by him.

That picture! To Tiki-Pu it seemed worth all the rest of the world put together. He knew, too, the story which was told of it, making it as holy to his eyes as the tombs of his own ancestors. The apprentices joked over it, calling it "Wio-Wani's back-door", "Wio-Wani's night-cap", and many other nicknames; but Tiki-Pu was quite sure, since the picture was so beautiful, that the story must be true.

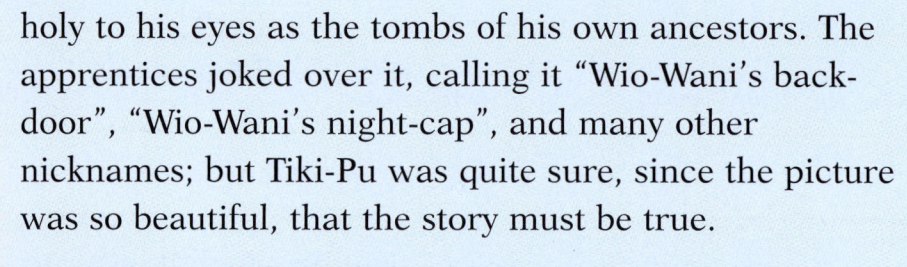

Wio-Wani, at the end of a long life, had painted it; a garden full of trees and sunlight, with high-standing flowers and green paths, and in their midst a palace. "The place where I would like to rest," said Wio-Wani, when it was finished.

So beautiful was it then, that the Emperor himself had come to see it; and gazing enviously at those peaceful walks, and the palace nestling among the trees, had sighed and owned that he too would be glad of such a resting-place. Then Wio-Wani stepped into the picture, and walked away along a path till he came, looking quite small and far off, to a low door in the palace-wall. Opening it, he turned and beckoned to the Emperor; but the Emperor did not follow; so Wio-Wani went in by himself, and shut the door between himself and the world for ever.

That happened three hundred years ago; but for Tiki-Pu the story was as fresh and true as if it had happened yesterday. When he was left to himself in the studio, all alone and locked up for the night, Tiki-Pu used to go and stare at the picture till it was too dark to see, and at the little palace with the door in its wall by which Wio-Wani had disappeared out of life. Then his soul would go down into his finger-tips, and he would knock softly and fearfully at the beautifully painted door, saying, "Wio-Wani, are you there?"

Little by little in the long-thinking nights, and the slow early mornings when light began to creep back through the papered windows of the studio, Tiki-Pu's soul became too much for him. He who could strain paper, and grind colours, and wash brushes, had everything within reach for becoming an artist, if it was the will of Fate that he should be one.

He began timidly at first, but in a little while he grew bold. With the first wash of light he was up from his couch on the hard floor and was daubing his soul out on scraps, and odds and ends, and stolen pieces of rice-paper.

Before long the short spell of daylight which lay between dawn and the arrival of the apprentices to their work did not suffice him. It took him so long to hide all traces of his doings, to wash out the brushes, and rinse clean the paint-pots he had used, and on the top of that to get the studio swept and dusted, that there was hardly time left him in which to indulge the itching of his fingers.

Driven by necessity, he became a pilferer of candle-ends, picking them from their sockets in the lanterns which the students carried on dark nights. Now and then one of these would remember that, when last used, his lantern had had a candle in it, and would accuse Tiki-Pu of having stolen it. "It is true," he would confess, "I was hungry – I have eaten it." The lie was so probable, he was believed easily, and was well beaten accordingly. Down in the ragged linings of his coat Tiki-Pu could hear the candle-ends rattling as the buffeting and chastisement fell upon him, and often he trembled lest his hoard should be discovered. But the truth of the matter never leaked out; and at night, as soon as he guessed that all the world outside was in bed, Tiki-Pu would mount one of his candles on a wooden stand and paint by the light of it, blinding himself over the task, till the dawn came and gave him a better and cheaper light to work by.

Tiki-Pu quite hugged himself over the results; he believed he was doing very well. "If only Wio-Wani were here to teach me," thought he, "I would be on the way to becoming a great painter!"

The resolution came to him one night that Wio-Wani should teach him. So he took a large piece of rice-paper and strained it, and sitting down opposite "Wio-Wani's back door", began painting. He had never set himself so big a task as this; by the dim stumbling light of his candle he strained his eyes nearly blind over the difficulties of it; and at last was almost driven to despair. How the trees stood row behind row, with air and sunlight between, and how the path went in and out, winding its way up to the little door in the palace-wall, were mysteries he could not fathom. He peered and peered and dropped tears into his paint-pots; but the secret of the mystery of such painting was far beyond him.

The door in the palace-wall opened; out came a little old man and began walking down the pathway towards him.

The soul of Tiki-Pu gave a sharp leap in his grubby little body. "That must be Wio-Wani himself and no other!" cried his soul.

Tiki-Pu pulled off his cap and threw himself down on the floor with reverent grovellings. When he dared to look up again Wio-Wani stood over him big and fine; just within the edge of the canvas he stood and reached out a hand.

"Come along with me, Tiki-Pu!" said the great one. "If you want to know how to paint I will teach you."

"Oh, Wio-Wani, were you there all the while?" cried Tiki-Pu ecstatically, leaping up and clutching with his smeary little puds the hand which the old man extended to him.

"I was there," said Wio-Wani, "looking at you out of my little window. Come along in!"

Tiki-Pu took a heave and swung himself into the picture, and fairly capered when he found his feet among the flowers of Wio-Wani's beautiful garden. Wio-Wani had turned, and was ambling gently back to the door of his palace, beckoning to the small one to follow him; and there stood Tiki-Pu opening his mouth like a fish to all the wonders that surrounded him. "Celestiality, may I speak?" he said suddenly.

"Speak," replied Wio-Wani; "what is it?"

"The Emperor, was he not the very flower of fools not to follow when you told him?"

"I cannot say," answered Wio-Wani, "but he certainly was no artist."

Then he opened the door, that door which he had so beautifully painted, and led Tiki-Pu in. Outside the little candle-end sat and guttered by itself, till the wick fell overboard, and the flame kicked itself out, leaving the studio in darkness and solitude to wait for the growings of another dawn.

It was full day before Tiki reappeared; he came running down the green path in great haste, jumped out of the frame on to the studio floor, and began tidying up his own messes of the night and the apprentices of the previous day. Only just in time did he have things ready by the hour when his master and the others returned to their work.

All that day they kept scratching their left ears, and could not think why; but Tiki-Pu knew, for he was saying over to himself all the things that Wio-Wani, the great painter, had been saying about them and their precious productions. And as he ground their colours for them and washed their brushes, and filled his famished little body with the breadcrumbs they threw away, little they guessed from what an immeasurable distance he looked down upon them all, and had Wio-Wani's word for it tickling his right ear all the day long.

Now before long Tiki-Pu's master noticed a change in him; and though he bullied him, and thrashed him, and did all that a careful master should do, he could not get the change out of him. So in a short while he grew suspicious. "What is the boy up to?" he wondered. "I have my eye on him all day: it must be at night that he gets into mischief."

It did not take Tiki-Pu's master a night's watching to find that something surreptitious was certainly going on. When it was dark he took up his post outside the studio, to see whether by any chance Tiki-Pu had some way of getting out; and before long he saw a faint light showing through the window. So he came and thrust his finger softly through one of the panes, and put his eye to the hole.

There inside was a candle burning on a stand, and Tiki-Pu squatting with paint-pots and brush in front of Wio-Wani's last masterpiece.

"What fine piece of burglary is this?" thought he; "what serpent have I been harbouring in my bosom? Is this beast of a grub of a boy thinking to make himself a painter and cut me out of my reputation and prosperity?" For even at that distance he could plainly perceive that the work of this boy went head and shoulders beyond his, or that of any painter living.

Presently Wio-Wani opened his door and came down the path, as was his habit now each night, to call Tiki-Pu to his lesson. He advanced to the front of the picture and beckoned for Tiki-Pu to come in with him; and Tiki-Pu's master grew clammy at the knees as he beheld Tiki-Pu catch hold of Wio-Wani's hand and jump into the picture, and skip up the green path by Wio-Wani's side, and in through the little door that Wio-Wani had painted so beautifully in the end wall of his palace!

For a time Tiki-Pu's master stood glued to the spot with grief and horror. "Oh, you deadly little underling! Oh, you poisonous little caretaker, you parasite, you vampire, you fly in amber!" cried he, "is that where you get your training? Is it there that you dare to go trespassing; into a picture that I purchased for my own pleasure and profit, and not at all for yours? Very soon we will see whom it really belongs to!"

He ripped out the paper of the largest window-pane and pushed his way through into the studio. Then in great haste he took up a paint-pot and brush, and sacrilegiously set himself to work upon Wio-Wani's last masterpiece. In the place of the doorway by which Tiki-Pu had entered he painted a solid brick wall; twice over he painted it, making it two bricks thick; brick by brick he painted it, and mortared every brick to its place. And when he had quite finished, he laughed, and called,

"Good night, Tiki-Pu!" and went home to be quite happy.

The next day all the apprentices were wondering what had become of Tiki-Pu; but as the master himself said nothing, and as another boy came to act as colour-grinder and brush-washer to the establishment, they very soon forgot all about him.

In the studio the master used to sit at work with his students all about him, and a mind full of ease and contentment. Now and then he would throw a glance across to the bricked-up doorway of Wio-Wani's palace, and laugh to himself, thinking how well he had served out Tiki-Pu for his treachery and presumption.

One day – it was five years after the disappearance of Tiki-Pu – he was giving his apprentices a lecture on the glories and the beauties and the wonders of Wio-Wani's painting – how nothing for colour could excel, or for mystery could equal it. To add point to his eloquence, he stood waving his hands before Wio-Wani's last masterpiece, and all his students and apprentices sat round him and looked.

Suddenly he stopped at mid-word, and broke off in the full flight of his eloquence, as he saw something like a hand come and take down the top brick from the face of paint which he had laid over the little door in the palace-wall which Wio-Wani had so beautifully painted. In another moment there was no doubt about it; brick by brick the wall was being pulled down, in spite of its double thickness.

The lecturer was altogether too dumbfounded and terrified to utter a word. He and all his apprentices stood round and stared while the demolition of the wall proceeded. Before long he recognized Wio-Wani with his flowing white beard; it was his handiwork this pulling down of the wall! He still had a brick in his hand when he stepped through the opening that he had made, and close after him stepped Tiki-Pu!

Tiki-Pu had grown tall and strong – he was even handsome; but for all that his old master recognized him, and saw with an envious foreboding that under his arms he carried many rolls and stretchers and portfolios, and other belongings of his craft. Clearly Tiki-Pu was coming back into the world, and was going to be a great painter.

Down the garden path came Wio-Wani, and Tiki-Pu walked after him; Tiki-Pu was so tall that his head stood well over Wio-Wani's shoulders – old man and young man together made a handsome pair.

How big Wio-Wani grew as he walked down the avenue of his garden and into the foreground of his picture! and how big the brick in his hand! and ah, how angry he seemed!

Wio-Wani came right down to the edge of the picture-frame and held up the brick. "What did you do that for?" he asked.

"I . . . didn't" Tiki-Pu's old master was beginning to reply; and the lie was still rolling on his tongue when the weight of the brick-bat, which he himself had reared, became his own tombstone.

Just inside the picture-frame stood Tiki-Pu, kissing the wonderful hands of Wio-Wani, which had taught him all their skill. "Good-bye, Tiki-Pu!"

said Wio-Wani, embracing him tenderly. "Now I am sending my second self into the world. When you are tired and want rest, come back to me: old Wio-Wani will take you in."

Tiki-Pu was sobbing and the tears were running down his cheeks as he stepped out of Wio-Wani's wonderfully painted garden and stood once more upon earth. Turning, he saw the old man walking away along the path towards the little door under the palace-wall. At the door Wio-Wani turned and waved his hand for the last time. Tiki-Pu still stood watching him. Then the door opened and shut, and Wio-Wani was gone. Softly as a flower the picture seemed to have folded its leaves over him.

Tiki-Pu leaned a wet face against the picture and kissed the door in the palace-wall which Wio-Wani had painted so beautifully. "Oh Wio-Wani, dear master," he cried, "are you there?"

He waited, and called again, but no voice answered him.

The Girl Who Stayed for Half a Week

by Gene Kemp

Nobody much noticed her come. Except for me and Miss. Nobody much noticed her go. Except for Miss and me. And that wasn't because of *her* but because I always noticed Miss. I liked to watch her. She reminded me of something – someone – somewhere, I couldn't quite remember, like the dream that slithers away out of reach when you wake in the morning and no matter how you try to bring it back it vanishes for good. Not that Miss was going to disappear, varromph, gone (I hope). Or like that feeling that pulls you round the next corner just to see what's beyond, or run to the top of the hill when you can hardly get your breath because there might, there just possibly might be something fabulous, fantastic, amazing, strange, wonderful, waiting there, just out of sight, on the other side. That was just the feeling Miss gave me.

Some kids hate their teacher. I nearly hated Mrs Baker last year. She always put me down. Look where you're putting your feet, Michael, must your work be so untidy, so messy, Michael, do you have to take up so much room, Michael? I couldn't help being me and sprouting in all directions. I couldn't help growing. I didn't tell myself to grow. I just did. But in the end I didn't hate her, there being other things to think about. In fact I gave her a box of chocolates at the end of the year, though I didn't choose my favourites and five other kids gave her the same kind.

But Miss is something else. If Miss reads something you've written and she thinks it's good she smiles at the pages before she says anything as if she understands the meaning behind the words you wrote on the page, sad or frightening or funny. She's got grey eyes and curly brown hair and a curly grin with a crooked tooth and she's not very big so I reach things down from the shelves for her, being the tallest in the class though Greg Grubber is wider. Maybe that's because my Dad's gynormous and feeds me on super grub (he's a great cook) or because he made me go to aikido classes and I'm a blue belt now. "It'll help to stop you putting your great big hoofs everywhere and smashing everything," he said. That was after Mum died, and I didn't know whether I was crashing and smashing everywhere because of my feet or because there was just a big black hole that I kept falling into no matter what I did. But that's not what this story's about . . .

It's about a girl who came and went and changed my life without knowing. I don't suppose I'll ever see her again to thank her, or even say hello. She came into our classroom in the middle of a Monday afternoon. I'd just looked up from the project I was doing (on oil) and there she stood by Miss's desk, a kind of smudge of a girl like a crayon drawing that Grubber might walk past and rub into rubbish with his elbow if he felt in the mood for a spot of aggro.

This girl looked as if someone had made quite a good job of her in the first place and then some toe-rag such as Grubber had rubbed her over, leaving her little and tired and pale and a bit dirty with a light turned off somewhere. Everyone in the room seemed busy – the projects were to be handed in by Tuesday – so I was the only one watching as Miss talked to her, because I'd looked up to see if Miss was OK.

You're saying, are you out of your tiny deformed mind, then? You might be big in the body but you've obviously got a brain the size of a pea. Look, idiot face, your teacher's supposed to look after you, not the other way round, OK. And yeah, we know you lost your mum, sorry, that was bad, but does it have to mean you have to mooch round after your teachers like a camel with a toothache?

I know all that, me, Michael Haines, I know all about it. So you can just leave the preaching and accept that I raised my eyes and saw this deprived-looking kid drooping by Miss's desk as if she'd rather be anywhere else at all in the whole world, even if it meant being dead or something. Miss was smiling at her as she does and I know she'd be asking her name, and how old, and did she like reading and so on. I've heard her with other new kids. She was welcoming, smiling at her as if she was wonderful, all smudgy as she was – the kid, not Miss.

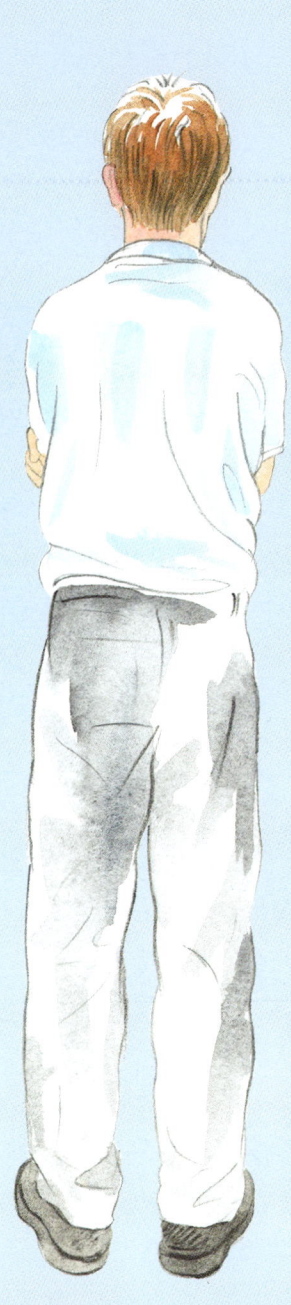

So I decided I'd wander up to that desk to borrow the stapler. Not that I needed the stapler just then but it made a good excuse. We've only got one in the classroom and you have to ask for it ever since Grubber tried to staple one of the mice from the Environment Area to a piece of card. When I got to the desk I heard Miss say, "You needn't read to me this afternoon if you're tired." And this girl, who just about came up to my knees, making me wonder what she was doing in our class (one of four top-year ones) gazed into Miss's face, then put down her head so her tatty hair fell everywhere, climbed on to Miss's knee, stuck her thumb in her mouth and her head on Miss's shoulder.

Now I knew I'd got to conceal this awful sight from some of our class members – Grubber not being the only one with a Heavy Metal inside – so I positioned myself between them and the class. Then Miss put her gently down, but still holding her hand, stood up and told all of us to put our things away.

"We'll have a story and a poem for the end of the afternoon," she said.

So we did. She read to us about a boy who went into a garden at midnight and what he found there. We sat and listened, even Grubber. He enjoys stories more than he admits.

"Anything's better than work, dog's breath," he says.

The girl hadn't yet got a seat to sit down on. She stood by Miss, holding her baggy sweater as if she might fly straight off Planet Earth if she let go, or sink down beneath the school, through the foundations and the rocks below, right down to the fiery centre of the planet. After a few minutes she climbed back on to Miss's knee, stuck her thumb in her mouth and her head on Miss's shoulder and this time stayed there as if she'd arrived home and wasn't leaving it, ever. Funnily enough, no one took any notice, as if they were just too lost in the story and she was part of it.

Next day she came late and was given her desk and books and so on. Later Miss heard her read and checked her maths and writing etc at her desk. And as we did our work she stayed there as if she never wanted to leave that place. At playtime I got ready to flatten Grubber if he started any of his funnies but there was no need. She stayed in. So did Miss, and anyone else who wished.

At the end of the afternoon, after clearing up, Miss brought out the story. The girl climbed on to her lap and held her as before.

On the fourth day Grubber at last registered she was there and went up to where she was doing her work at the side of Miss's desk. Miss was with a group in the far corner of the room.

"What's all this, then?" asked Grubber, in a voice like a Rottweiler with laryngitis. "How come you gits doin' your rubbish 'ere. You ain't no special right 'ere. Git lost, vomit."

Now Grubber and me, we've always scrapped. Yes, all the way up from toddler group, playgroup, Infants and through to the Middle. We fought at two, three, four, five, six, seven, eight, then at nine I started to go to aikido. After that he couldn't win any more though that didn't stop him trying. No style, though, no discipline, only size and power. Yeah, Grubber's got that. Power.

And he intended using it. He meant to turf out little Smudge from her safe place by Miss's chair. He fancied doing that. Not that he wanted to be there himself, oh no, the further he was from any teacher the better, but if this new kid wanted to be there that wouldn't do. Grubber couldn't have that. He got ready to move her.

But I was there first.

"She can work here if she wants to."

"What's with you, snail slime?"

We were both shouting in whispers now . . .

"Leave her alone."

"Get lost, sewer."

. . . in case Miss heard. If she hadn't been in the room

there would've been a scrap but –

The sound of feet running down the corridor outside.

A scream.

Another scream. "Stop him!"

A bell. A buzzer. "Ring the police!"

More running feet.

More screams. Louder now. And louder.

The door burst open. Miss stood up and came out of her corner.

The woman who'd rushed in, white, scared, looked round, ran to little Smudge by the desk, grabbed her and raced *behind* Miss.

"Save me! Save me!" she was babbling.

A man burst in, as red as she was white, big, angry, bald, shirtsleeves flapping.

Miss held out her arms.

"Stop!" she cried.

He went to shove her aside.

"I'm going to get you. You're coming home with me," he shouted, and pushed Miss away. She crashed into a desk.

My stomach did a freefall.

So among the shouts, the screams, the bangs, I looked at Grubber and Grubber nodded back. Like friends for ever

249

and always we moved in. Grubber chopped him in the back. I high-kicked him just where it hurts.

He went down and we sat on him. So did half the class as into the room poured the school secretary, the head teacher, several helpers and most of the other fourth years.

The head teacher hauled the man to his feet. He looked a bit shattered, as well he might. There seemed to be hundreds of people in our classroom as the police arrived. And then the woman threw her arms round him and he put his arms round her. They were both crying. In the confusion I think only two people noticed little Smudge slip out of the room. Me and Miss. Miss called out and I tried to follow but there were too many people and too much noise.

The next day was Friday. At the end of it Miss went on with *Tom's Midnight Garden*. We sat quiet and subdued. The girl hadn't appeared. At the end of the afternoon I went up to Miss where she sat looking as sad as she had that time Julie Trent had asked why she wasn't wearing her pretty ring any more. Things didn't work out, that's why, Julie, she'd said, things don't always work out.

"Why didn't that girl come?" I asked.

"Oh, she won't be coming here any more. She was staying at the Refuge, but they've all gone back home now. A good thing, I expect. I hope." She didn't sound at all sure.

"You liked her a lot, didn't you, Miss?"

"Yes, I did. Well, it's Friday, Michael, and time to go."

My father stood at the door. He hadn't been into school so far this term because of his working hours. He strode towards Miss.

"I had to come to see you," he said to her, "to see what really happened yesterday. I heard a most extraordinary story from Michael. I haven't seen him so upset for ages."

She told him, but it seemed to me that what they were really doing was looking at each other as if they'd just seen a miracle, and what they were saying wasn't all that important.

Somebody nudged me.

"You comin', then? Thought you might like to try out me new bike."

It was Grubber. We ran out together.

Oh yeah, they got married, my dad and Miss, some time later, when I'd gone to my next school with my mate Grubber.

As a mum she's not the dream round the corner or the something fantastic on the other side of the hill, but she's OK. She'll do. Sometimes she gets a funny look though, and I get this odd feeling that she's remembering the girl who only stayed for half a week and looked as if she'd been smudged.

Author Index

Ahlberg, Allan *Please Mrs Butler*	118
Ahlberg, Allan *Colin*	116
Ahlberg, Allan *Sometimes God*	186
Ahlberg, Allan *The Gang*	185
Ahlberg, Allan *I Did a Bad Thing Once*	184
Aiken, Joan *A Necklace of Raindrops*	204
Aiken, Joan *Lost - One Pair of Legs*	194
Akinrele, Joni *BED!*	171
Anon *The Panther Roars*	89
Anon *My Bonnie*	87
Anon *Eskimo Lullaby*	82
Anon *Praise song of the Wind*	88
Anon *A Schoolmaster's Admonition*	119
Anon *Riddles in Rhyme*	168
Anon *Jelly on the Plate*	169
Anon *Demeanour*	120
Anon *Quartermaster's Stores*	84
Avery, Heather & Cwardi, Anne *The Knowhow Book of Print and Paint*	128
Barrett, Norman *Whales*	110
Bateson, David *Crown of Light Festival*	77
Berry, James *Isn't My Name Magical*	159
Bloom, Valerie *Chicken Dinner*	161
Brand, Dionne *Hurricane*	159
Burgess, Gelett *Limerick*	189
Charles, Faustin *Brazilian Footballer*	158
Cook, Stanley *In the Playground*	184
Cunliffe, John *Orders of the Day*	12
Dahl, Roald *Centipede's Song*	172
Fisher, Aileen *Light the Festive Candles*	76
Graves, Robert *Allie*	86
Greaves, Margaret *Once there were no Pandas*	152
Higgins, Beatrice *My Gerbil*	187
Hooper, Mary *Spook Spotting*	90
Houseman, Laurence *A Chinese Fairy Tale*	228
Hughes, Ted *Autumn Song*	6
Isherwood, Shirley *William's Problems*	16
Jackson, Wayne *Anne Frank*	52
Jaffrey, Madhur *Savitri and Satyavan*	138
Jones, Terry *A Fish of the World*	112
Kemp, Gene *The Girl Who Stayed for Half a Week*	242
Kerr, Judith *When Hitler Stole Pink Rabbit*	58
Kingfisher *Fish*	108
Klein, Robin *Hey, Danny!*	176
Lewis, Marcus *WHY?*	175
Magee, Wes *A Green Harvest*	46
Mare, Walter de la *The Dunce*	121
Milne, A.A. *The Good Little Girl*	82
Mungoshi, Charles *The Slave who became Chief*	216
Nottridge, Rhoda *Let's Celebrate Winter*	72
Oldfield, Pamela *The Not-Very-Nice-Prince*	132
Palin, Michael *Limerick*	189
Powling, Chris *The Conker as Hard as a Diamond*	96
Robinson, Catherine *Mog and Bumble*	8
Rosen, Michael *If you don't put your Shoes On*	14
Rosen, Michael *The Outing*	121
Rosen, Michael *Eddie and the Gerbils*	190
Rosen, Michael *Juster and Waiter*	13
Siliprandi, Katerini & Watson, Sheila *Tudors and Stuarts*	22
Sheldon, Dyan *Seymour Finds a Home*	78
Shreve, Susan *Cheating*	162
Stillie, Margaret *Haiku*	172
Usborne *Fishing Boats*	106
Williams, David *Leave me Alone*	38
Zolotow, Charlotte *River Winding*	7

253

Acknowledgements

The editor and publishers wish to thank the following for permission to use copyright material:

Academic Books (Pvt) Ltd, incorporating Baobab Books, for Charles Mungoshi, 'The Slave who became chief' from *Stories from a Shona Childhood*, Baobab Books;

David Bateson for 'Crown of Light Festival' Copyright © 1989 by David Bateson;

Carcanet Press Ltd for Robert Graves, 'Allie' from *Complete Poems*;

Curtis Brown (Aust) Pty Ltd, on behalf of Haytul Pty Ltd for Robin Klein, 'Hey Danny' from *Ratbags and Rascals*;

Egmont Children's Books Ltd for Margaret Greaves, *Once There Were No Pandas*, Methuen Children's Books (1985); and A.A.Milne, 'The Good Little Girl' from *Now We Are Six*, Methuen Children's Books:

Faber & Faber for Gene Kemp, 'The Girl who stayed for half a week' from *Roundabout* (1993), and Ted Hughes, 'There came a day' from *Season Songs*;

Aileen Fisher for 'Light the Festive Candles' from *Skip Around the Year* (Thomas Y.Crowell). Copyright © 1967 by Aileen Fisher. Reprinted by permission of Harper & Row Publishers Inc.

A M Heath & Co Ltd on behalf of the author for Joan Aiken, 'A Necklace of Raindrops' from *A Necklace of Raindrops and Other Stories*, Puffin (1975). © Joan Aiken Enterprises Ltd 1968 and 'Lost – One Pair of Legs' from *The Last Slice of Rainbow*, Puffin (1988). © Joan Aiken Enterprises Ltd 1985;

David Higham Associates on behalf of the Estate of the author for Roald Dahl, 'The Centipede's Song' from *James and the Giant Peach*, Penguin; and on behalf of the author for John Cunliffe, 'Orders of the Day' included in *A Second Poetry Book*, compiled by John Foster, Oxford University Press;

Judith Kerr for 'When Hitler Stole Pink Rabbit' © Judith Kerr (1971);

Kingfisher for material from *First Encyclopedia*, pp.56-57. © Larousse Plc 1996;

The Literary Trustees of Walter de la Mare, and the Society of Authors as their representative for 'The Dunce' from *The Complete Poems of Walter de la Mare* (1969);

Wes Magee for 'A Green Harvest';

Mary Maggs for 'My Gerbil' by Beatrice Higgins © Mary Maggs, 1998;

Pamela Oldfield for 'The Not-Very-Nice-Prince' from *Naughty Stories*;

Pavillion Books for Madhur Jaffrey, 'Savitri and Satyavan' from *Seasons of Splendour* (1985) pp. 9-17; and Terry Jones, 'A Fish of the World' from *Fairy Tales* (1981);

Penguin Books Ltd for Allan Ahlberg, 'Please Mrs Butler' (pp.10-11), 'I did a Bad Thing Once' (pp. 38), 'The Gang' (pp.40-41), 'Sometimes God' (pp.46-47) and 'Colin' (pp.46-47) from *Please Mrs Butler* (Kestrel, 1983). © Allan Ahlberg, 1983; and material from Chris Powling, *The Conker as Hard as a Diamond* (Kestrel Books, 1984) pp. 5-7, 45-59. © Chris Powling, 1984;

The Peters Fraser and Dunlop Group Ltd on behalf of the author for Michael Rosen, 'You Put Your Shoes On' from *Mind Your Own Business*, Andre Deutsch, and Michael Rosen, 'Juster and Waiter' from *A Second Poetry Book*, compiled by John Foster, Oxford University Press, 'Eddie and the Gerbils' from *Quick Let's Get Out of Here*, Puffin (1985), © Michael Rosen (1983) and 'The Outing' from *The Hypnotiser*;

Random House UK for Laurence Houseman, 'A Chinese Fairy Tale' from *Moonshine and Clover*, Jonathan Cape;

Russell ans Volkening, Inc on behalf of the author for Susan Shreve, 'Cheating' from *Family Secrets*, Alfred A Knopf, Inc. © 1979 by Susan Shreve;

Usborne Publishing Ltd. for material from *The Usborne First Book of Knowledge* p45 and *The KnowHow Book of Print and Paint* p2 © Usborne Publishing Ltd;

Walker Books Ltd for 'Spook Spotting'. Text © 1993 Mary Hooper from SPOOK SPOTTING illustrated by Susan Hellard. Reproduced by permission of the publisher Walker Books Ltd., London:

Franklin Watts for 'Whales' from WHALES, by Norman Barrett, first published in the UK by Franklin Watts, a division of the Watts Publishing Group, 96 Leonard Street, London, EC2A 4RH;

MacDonald Publishers for 'Williams Problems' by Shirley Isherwood from *The First Storybook Collection*, 'Seymour Finds a Home' by Dyan Sheldon from *The Second Storybook Collection* and 'Mog and Bumble' by Catherine Robinson from *The Third Storybook Collection*;

Wayland Publishers for material from *Elizabeth I* by Sheila Watson, *Anne Frank (Life Stories)* by Wayne Jackson, *Henry VIII* by Katerini Siliprandi and *Let's Celebrate Winter* by Rhoda Nottridge;

David Williams for 'Leave me Alone';

Every effort has been made to trace the copyright holders but if any have been inadvertently overlooked the publishers will be pleased to make the necessary arrangements at the first opportunity.

Illustrations © STP, by:

Jeffrey Burn, Debbie Clarke, Abigail Conway, Jacqueline East, Michael Evans, Emma Garner, Jane Gerwitz, Diana Gold, Nick Hawken, Sarah Hedley, George Hollingworth, Susan Hutchison, Michelle Ives, Nadine Faye James, Linda Jeffrey, Bethan Matthews, Isobelle Morgan-Giles, Jill Newton, Patti Pearce, Rhiannon Powell, Jeffrey Reid, Linda Scott, Jane Smith, Lisa Williams